Jean Baudrillard

Titles in the series Critical Lives present the work of leading cultural figures of the modern period. Each book explores the life of the artist, writer, philosopher or architect in question and relates it to their major works.

In the same series

Hannah Arendt *Samantha Rose Hill*
Antonin Artaud *David A. Shafer*
John Ashbery *Jess Cotton*
Roland Barthes *Andy Stafford*
Georges Bataille *Stuart Kendall*
Charles Baudelaire *Rosemary Lloyd*
Jean Baudrillard *Emmanuelle Fantin and Bran Nicol*
Simone de Beauvoir *Ursula Tidd*
Samuel Beckett *Andrew Gibson*
Walter Benjamin *Esther Leslie*
John Berger *Andy Merrifield*
Leonard Bernstein *Paul R. Laird*
Joseph Beuys *Claudia Mesch*
Jorge Luis Borges *Jason Wilson*
Constantin Brancusi *Sanda Miller*
Bertolt Brecht *Philip Glahn*
Charles Bukowski *David Stephen Calonne*
Mikhail Bulgakov *J.A.E. Curtis*
William S. Burroughs *Phil Baker*
Byron *David Ellis*
John Cage *Rob Haskins*
Albert Camus *Edward J. Hughes*
Fidel Castro *Nick Caistor*
Paul Cézanne *Jon Kear*
Coco Chanel *Linda Simon*
Noam Chomsky *Wolfgang B. Sperlich*
Jean Cocteau *James S. Williams*
Joseph Conrad *Robert Hampson*
H.D. (Hilda Doolittle) *Lara Vetter*
Salvador Dalí *Mary Ann Caws*
Charles Darwin *J. David Archibald*
Guy Debord *Andy Merrifield*
Claude Debussy *David J. Code*
Gilles Deleuze *Frida Beckman*
Fyodor Dostoevsky *Robert Bird*
Marcel Duchamp *Caroline Cros*
Sergei Eisenstein *Mike O'Mahony*
Frantz Fanon *James S. Williams*
William Faulkner *Kirk Curnutt*
Gustave Flaubert *Anne Green*
Ford Madox Ford *Max Saunders*
Michel Foucault *David Macey*
Benjamin Franklin *Kevin J. Hayes*
Sigmund Freud *Matthew ffytche*
Mahatma Gandhi *Douglas Allen*
Antoni Gaudí *Michael Eaude*
Jean Genet *Stephen Barber*
Allen Ginsberg *Steve Finbow*
Johann Wolfgang von Goethe *Jeremy Adler*
Günter Grass *Julian Preece*
Ernest Hemingway *Verna Kale*
E.T.A. Hoffmann *Ritchie Robertson*
Langston Hughes *W. Jason Miller*
Victor Hugo *Bradley Stephens*
Zora Neale Hurston *Cheryl R. Hopson*
Aldous Huxley *Jake Poller*
J.-K. Huysmans *Ruth Antosh*
Christopher Isherwood *Jake Poller*
Derek Jarman *Michael Charlesworth*
Alfred Jarry *Jill Fell*
James Joyce *Andrew Gibson*
Carl Jung *Paul Bishop*
Franz Kafka *Sander L. Gilman*

Frida Kahlo *Gannit Ankori*
Søren Kierkegaard *Alastair Hannay*
Yves Klein *Nuit Banai*
Arthur Koestler *Edward Saunders*
Akira Kurosawa *Peter Wild*
D. H. Lawrence *David Ellis*
Lenin *Lars T. Lih*
Jack London *Kenneth K. Brandt*
Pierre Loti *Richard M. Berrong*
Rosa Luxemburg *Dana Mills*
Jean-François Lyotard *Kiff Bamford*
René Magritte *Patricia Allmer*
Gustav Mahler *Stephen Downes*
Stéphane Mallarmé *Roger Pearson*
Thomas Mann *Herbert Lehnert and Eva Wessell*
Gabriel García Márquez *Stephen M. Hart*
Karl Marx *Paul Thomas*
Henri Matisse *Kathryn Brown*
Guy de Maupassant *Christopher Lloyd*
Herman Melville *Kevin J. Hayes*
Henry Miller *David Stephen Calonne*
Yukio Mishima *Damian Flanagan*
Eadweard Muybridge *Marta Braun*
Vladimir Nabokov *Barbara Wyllie*
Pablo Neruda *Dominic Moran*
Friedrich Nietzsche *Ritchie Robertson*
Georgia O'Keeffe *Nancy J. Scott*
Richard Owen *Patrick Armstrong*
Octavio Paz *Nick Caistor*
Fernando Pessoa *Bartholomew Ryan*
Pablo Picasso *Mary Ann Caws*
Edgar Allan Poe *Kevin J. Hayes*
Ezra Pound *Alec Marsh*
Sergei Prokofiev *Christina Guillaumier*
Marcel Proust *Adam Watt*
Sergei Rachmaninoff *Rebecca Mitchell*
Maurice Ravel *Emily Kilpatrick*
Arthur Rimbaud *Seth Whidden*
John Ruskin *Andrew Ballantyne*
Jean-Paul Sartre *Andrew Leak*
Erik Satie *Mary E. Davis*
Arnold Schoenberg *Mark Berry*
Arthur Schopenhauer *Peter B. Lewis*
Dmitry Shostakovich *Pauline Fairclough*
Adam Smith *Jonathan Conlin*
Susan Sontag *Jerome Boyd Maunsell*
Gertrude Stein *Lucy Daniel*
Stendhal *Francesco Manzini*
Igor Stravinsky *Jonathan Cross*
Rabindranath Tagore *Bashabi Fraser*
Pyotr Tchaikovsky *Philip Ross Bullock*
Dylan Thomas *John Goodby and Chris Wigginton*
Leo Tolstoy *Andrei Zorin*
Leon Trotsky *Paul Le Blanc*
Mark Twain *Kevin J. Hayes*
Richard Wagner *Raymond Furness*
Alfred Russel Wallace *Patrick Armstrong*
Simone Weil *Palle Yourgrau*
Tennessee Williams *Paul Ibell*
Ludwig Wittgenstein *Edward Kanterian*
Virginia Woolf *Ira Nadel*
Frank Lloyd Wright *Robert McCarter*

Jean Baudrillard

Emmanuelle Fantin and Bran Nicol

REAKTION BOOKS

For Isaac, unknowingly Baudrillardian, and James,
who has a sharp eye for simulation

Published by Reaktion Books Ltd
2–4 Sebastian Street
London EC1V 0HE, UK

www.reaktionbooks.co.uk

First published 2025
Copyright © Emmanuelle Fantin and Bran Nicol 2025

EU GPSR Authorised Representative
Logos Europe, 9 rue Nicolas Poussin, 17000, La Rochelle, France
email: contact@logoseurope.eu

Printed and bound in Great Britain by Bell & Bain, Glasgow

A catalogue record for this book is available from the British Library

ISBN 978 1 83639 103 6

Contents

Introduction: The Disappearance of Jean Baudrillard   7

1   Belonging and Breaking Away, 1929–66   20

2   Objects and Objections, 1966–70   39

3   Becoming 'Baudrillard': Seductions and Provocations, 1970–79   59

4   Life on the Other Side: Art and America, 1980–86   80

5   'My own strange world': Baudrillard's Alternative 1980s   98

6   Total Freedom, 1990–2004   116

Conclusion: Beyond   141

References   155
Select Bibliography   176
Acknowledgements   181
Photo Acknowledgements   182

Introduction: The Disappearance of Jean Baudrillard

> One day the only people left on the streets will be zombies – one
> group with their mobile phones, the other with their headphones
> or video headsets. Everyone will be simultaneously elsewhere. They
> already are. In the past, you could isolate yourself internally. Now
> you can isolate yourself externally, can retreat into the outer core of
> your being.[1]

In November 2005, less than two years before the end of his life and
during a period when his status as 'extremely famous cult figure' was
at its height, Jean Baudrillard gave a reading at the Tilton Gallery on
East 76th Street in New York. The reading was to promote his book
The Conspiracy of Art, which had just been published. But soon the
discussion veered away from art and on to the celebrity status of
Baudrillard himself. A member of the audience spoke up:

> You're Baudrillard, and you were able to fill a room. And what I
> want to know is: when someone dies, we read an obituary – like
> Derrida died last year, and is a great loss for all of us. What would
> you like to be said about you? In other words, who are you? I
> would like to know how old you are, if you're married and if you
> have kids, and since you've spent a great deal of time writing a
> great many books, some of which I could not get through, is there
> something you want to say that can be summed up?

Baudrillard responded: 'What I am, I don't know. I am the
simulacrum of myself.'[2]

Jean Baudrillard in 1987.

At first glance, his answer seems a playful attempt to dodge biographical scrutiny. But in fact he was being honest. The simulacrum – that which comes to stand in for something real, and with which we engage *as if it is real* – was perhaps Baudrillard's key concept. His public persona, as embodiment of the iconic, enigmatic French theorist, a category of thinker which had become something of a French export commodity since the last decades of the twentieth century, inevitably had to stand in for his real self, the person who wrote his books.[3] This separation between real self and the self constructed by and for the public is a consequence of publicity that all famous writers and thinkers have to deal with. But it also connects to something that lies at the very heart of Baudrillard's thinking. Simulation, the production of simulacra, causes the real to disappear. Baudrillard spent a lifetime pointing this out, occasionally in exasperation at being misunderstood, but usually deriving enjoyment from the provocation it caused.

In the last two decades before he died Baudrillard had increasingly been turning his thoughts to his own 'disappearance'. In 1990 he acknowledged he belonged to a generation of influential French philosophers, which included contemporaries like Jean-François Lyotard and Jacques Derrida, who he felt were 'living well from philosophy'. The aim was not to keep doing well by continuing to publish books or to lecture. It was 'to work oneself out fully and then disappear', to practice disappearance as 'an art form, a seductive way of leaving the world'.[4] 'Part of disappearing', Baudrillard said, 'is to disappear before you die, to disappear before you have run dry, while you still have something to say.'[5] This was a rare achievement. Lyotard and Derrida (who would eventually die before he did, in 1998 and 2004 respectively) were not so caught up in the process of disappearance. Andy Warhol, by contrast, died at just the moment he should have died. For Baudrillard this was more than just a matter of bowing out at the right time but one closely aligned to the key principles of his philosophy.

Writing the critical life of Baudrillard is also the chronicling of a subtle yet persistent and deliberate practice of disappearing. We turn to critical biographies of artists and thinkers hoping to gain a clearer view of their work by discovering little pieces of the individual behind it, from remarks or confessions they made, or anecdotes about their public, daily life. The life of Jean Baudrillard makes finding connections between his biography and his work difficult. So much seems to have been left unsaid. His aesthetics (which is also perhaps an ethics) of disappearance meant he cultivated a persona that was intended to be mysterious and enigmatic, to preserve the impression that his work was separate from himself in an autobiographical sense, and to make it difficult to draw connections between his life and his work. No modern figure who produced such a substantial opus of books and articles, was internationally renowned for decades, and spent his whole life expressing himself in journals, in interviews, at conferences and in a wealth of media contributions, not even Derrida, was able to remain so singular, enigmatic and resistant to categorization. To maintain such an *absence* within such a public life is almost miraculous.

Baudrillard made copious personal notes and fragments throughout his life. Initially these were scribbled on random papers not intended for publication, but eventually they became five volumes of a series called *Cool Memories* spanning 1980 to 2005. Public record contains glimpses of a more enigmatic and eccentric individual: a man who reputedly faked the artist Sophie Calle's diploma 'to help her escape round the world'; who read his poetry at a 'philosophy-rave' in a casino in Stateline, Nevada, in 1996 backed by art musicians The Chance Band; who did not turn up to a party because he was watching reruns of *Wheel of Fortune* on TV; and who once met the translator David Macey at the Compendium bookshop in London 'wearing a thick full-length coat on an extremely hot summer's day, reading one of his works in translation while laughing loudly'.[6] He said of the *Cool Memories* series, 'There is no reason to hide a mirror in one's own drawer.'[7] But even though these fragments were published, the man behind the reflection remained hidden. What might be personal is presented in a curiously impersonal way. Take this note, for example: 'Everything makes us impatient. Perhaps we feel remorse for a life which is too long, from the point of view of the species, for the use we make of it.'[8] Is he really speaking for himself here? He played upon this uncertainty, stating elsewhere that 'he who speaks of himself should never say the whole truth; he should keep it secret and divulge only fragments.'[9] Baudrillard was also a gifted photographer who left an abundance of pictures, which are still regularly exhibited all over the world, but these, too, tell us little directly about himself.

Privacy, camouflage and making sure he was forgotten were established as such cardinal virtues in Baudrillard's public persona that it made the game of playing 'hide and seek' – using snippets of information about his own biography and personality, seeking 'the secret side' of Baudrillard – pointless. This has been acknowledged by others who have written about Baudrillard. Serge Latouche stated that when it came to Baudrillard, 'writing a *real* biography is *hyper* impossible.'[10] Gary Genosko, in his anthology *Uncollected Baudrillard*, insisted that even though his book is about uncovering a hitherto un-anthologized trove of essays by Baudrillard (a project about which Baudrillard said he was 'nonplussed'), it could not be mistaken for an exercise in uncovering 'secrets' about their author because: 'There is nothing to be revealed about the identity of Baudrillard that was not already known in one way or another.'[11]

Our view is that exploring the fragments is the ideal first step into Baudrillard's life and work – precisely because they are still a mystery, buried in his carefully constructed forgetfulness. His commitment to fragmentary writing, and his determination to erase his biography, are not just stylistic decisions but are typical of Baudrillard himself. It is not an accident that although 'the real' is the core concept examined throughout his books, the 'real' Baudrillard remains a riddle. In *Cool Memories IV* he notes 'the real is born of lack of imagination.'[12] Imagination turns what is real into what is unreal, or – in Baudrillard's terminology – into a simulacrum. In the pages that follow we suggest that it is precisely here, in the blurred zone between reality and imagination, that the connection between life and writing is to be found. Our aim is not to construct an imaginary, simulated Baudrillard, nor to pretend to be able to capture the 'essence' of Baudrillard, but to stick to the facts we know and to limit speculation – using where possible his own words – while respecting his convictions about intimacy, erasure, secrecy and disappearance, and enabling readers to decide for themselves who the real Baudrillard was.

Baudrillard is one of the most influential thinkers of our times, but his philosophy is among the most misunderstood. He cared little about labels or categories – and shrugged off any that were applied to him, resisting being pinned down to any specific movement, group or academic discipline, such as Marxism or postmodernism. When employed as a sociologist at the University of Nanterre he declared that there was no such thing as the 'social'. It was, one commentator later observed, 'a magnificently suicidal gesture for a practising sociologist'.[13] When, in the 1980s, he 'became a guru of postmodernism' Baudrillard wryly confessed he had had 'undeserved success based on a total misunderstanding'.[14] He disappointed the audience for a sell-out lecture at the Whitney Museum of American Art in New York in 1987 by asserting that contemporary art did not interest him and in any case art had disappeared. Although his influence on the 1999 film *The Matrix* (dir. Lana Wachowski and Lilly Wachowski) propelled him into a new kind of cult fame, he immediately dismissed the association with his ideas, protesting that it was 'the kind of film about the matrix that the matrix would have been able to produce'.[15] He felt his 'trajectory' always 'passed through' disciplines that wished to adopt him as one of their own – sociology, architecture, philosophy, art – without resting anywhere for long. 'For me,' he said, 'even the history of ideas is a field with which I flirt, at its limits, but I only pass through. I work more at a distance.'[16]

The image of Baudrillard as not being a 'joiner', preferring to remain a loner, will return several times in this volume. David Macey likened Baudrillard's stance to that of the 'dandy': 'cold and even cynical, he watches'.[17] He cultivated a kind of radicality of loneliness, brandishing it as a banner to be proud of. But as much as his resistance to belonging or being categorized is explained by his fierce independence, it is also a measure of his uncompromising commitment to his ideas and the way he understood the world. As much as he embodied the image of the enigmatic French theorist, his outsider persona meant he also transcended it. He was both more 'cool' than other famous French thinkers (chiefly because of the enthusiastic embrace of his ideas and spirit by the art world of

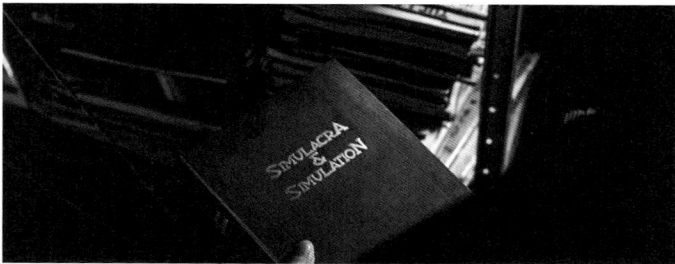

Neo hides a floppy disk inside a copy of *Simulacra and Simulation*, in *The Matrix* (1999; dir. the Wachowskis).

the 1980s and '90s) and, at the same time, more down to earth and humble. The film-maker and writer Chris Kraus said that when she met him in Paris in the late 1980s he 'wasn't rapacious or garrulous like the other French cultural figures we'd met . . . he seemed to not give a shit what anyone thought of him'.[18] It was not simply that Baudrillard cultivated the persona of a loner. He put it into practice, he lived it, preferring to engage with artists and cultural figures, and criticize and needle other philosophers (such as Michel Foucault) so that he remained outside the 'club' of French theory.[19]

Constructing explanatory narratives was entirely at odds with the principles and the practice of Baudrillard's writing. One of the fundamental characteristics of his thinking, there from his earliest years to the end, was his disbelief in the potential of any system of analysis or meaning-making (psychoanalysis, science, art history and so on) to capture the object of analysis accurately. He insisted that objects continually demonstrate their capacity to evade the grasp of any system that attempts to explain them. Trying to capture the essence of something – or someone – inevitably meant its reality became more elusive. Such is the paradox of the aesthetics of disappearance. The closer one gets to an object of scrutiny, the further it recedes into 'the real' and the more it becomes inaccessible directly. In fact, the object leads the subject (a term used in theory to refer to the individual human being) on, as if through an agency of its own.

Biography is one such system. It is geared towards explaining, valuing and accounting for parts of a life, ironing out idiosyncrasies and constructing a complete portrait of a singular individual. In Baudrillardian terms, the subject of a biography is in fact an object and this means that the object will confound the biographers and resist being fully explained. In keeping with this principle Baudrillard himself offered little commentary on the artistic and philosophical figures he most admired, though he would cite them in his writing. The work of artists and poets like Alfred Jarry, Antonin Artaud, Arthur Rimbaud and Friedrich Hölderlin, or philosophers such as Friedrich Nietzsche, were so 'secret' and 'singular' to him that he was reluctant to write too much about them.[20] He carefully kept his distance. Baudrillard's first essay on Artaud – who he would suggest was perhaps the most important influence of all – was written when he was 21, but not published until 55 years later. In his twenties he read Nietzsche 'exhaustively', but 'after that I never read Nietzsche again'.[21]

He nevertheless admired the ability of artists like Artaud, Hölderlin and Jarry to dissolve their life and personality into their art, and to exist 'in some sort of state of poetic grace'.[22] He attempted something similar. It was not just his life that he wanted to withdraw from view so the focus could remain on his writing. He wanted his writing itself to be seductive and elusive; to read like thought-provoking fragments that gestured towards a secret whole system behind them. He was not concerned that this meant he might not be fully understood or that readers would be frustrated. As he told the Italian visual artist Enrico Baj in the early 1990s, he favoured 'provocation' over 'invocation'. This meant actively seeking a 'negative or paradoxical abreaction' from those confronted by his ideas, rather than agreement or influence.[23] In his 1990s work especially, he thought of his object of study as 'extreme phenomena': wars, viruses, global events. Surely extreme phenomena require a provocative method to examine them, which should elicit extreme responses?

Baudrillard was very unlike Derrida, the philosopher famed most for the theory and method known as 'deconstruction'. Yet Baudrillard thought that his own method was also to 'destroy things just as they are being constructed'. This was not because of any 'deliberate, "subversive" will to deconstruct' but because he wanted to identify 'the mode in which things try to disappear'. The way to achieve this, he thought, was to surrender himself to writing. To write, he said, is to be at the very heart of the 'demand for a drive to disappearance and the power to bring it about'.[24]

His dedication to erase traces not just of himself but of his influences is such a feature of his books and articles that we can say that the absence of traces *is*, ironically, a distinctively 'Baudrillardian' lineament of his writings. Academic manuscripts are usually supplied with footnotes, quotations, sources and so

Baudrillard in Berlin, 1992.

on, but Baudrillard's books largely eschew precise and explicit references. There are few endnotes. This presents his readers with a challenge, because it means we have to trust him when he refers to this theory of Marx, such and such a comment by Nietzsche or a particular excerpt from Elias Canetti. To complicate things further Baudrillard admitted to mischievously inserting into his writing entirely fictitious quotations. His unwillingness to play the referencing game also conveys a self-confidence on his part. It means in his writing he espouses a liberty of speech which is more radical than that of conventionally 'rigorous' academic writings.

Baudrillard's commitment to the fragmentary and the provocative actually reveals another secret about his thought: it is in fact remarkably consistent. The more of Baudrillard one reads, the more one becomes convinced about this uniformity. Reading Baudrillard is like entering a complete system, one which works according to its own logic and its own rules. In one of his last books, there is an especially interesting statement, delivered impersonally but which reads unmistakably like a veiled confession about his own work:

> There is an original form of repetition, the one that translates the fact that one has but one idea in one's life (when one is lucky enough to have one), but that analysing it allows one to make it nuanced or to make it appear and reappear according to the form of the spiral or the anamorphosis.[25]

Calling Baudrillard a one-idea philosopher (even though he suggests it himself) does not do justice to the profundity and reach of his thinking, the sheer mass of ideas and events and cultural phenomena covered in the forty or so books he published, the innumerable essays and articles, the hundreds of interviews he gave. Yet his conviction about the disappearance of the real – as a result of modern systems continually producing what we experience as reality, or because of efforts to fully understand or explain something and the object eluding one's grasp – is the core idea upon which his work is founded. This idea spirals in and out of view as we read Baudrillard, taking different forms, renewing itself through a restlessly refreshed vocabulary.

The consistency of his philosophy means it is not possible to do what we can do with other thinkers and look for 'breaks' between different 'phases' of Baudrillard's thought. His earlier work is closer to more conventional academic analysis, while the later work – from the publication of *Seduction* in 1979 – is more elliptical, enigmatic and compulsive. Yet his work overall is best understood as an effort to explore the same set of preoccupations through different lenses rather than as a system that went through distinct stages or developed as a result of decisive changes of direction. Baudrillard himself seems never to have accepted that there may be divisions between earlier and later phases in his life. When asked how old he was by a member of the audience at the Tilton Gallery reading in New York in 2005, the 76-year-old Baudrillard replied 'very young'.[26]

Baudrillard's writing is just as carefully elusive as his biography. In fact, the two are as one; his life was lived so as to remain true to the convictions in his books. Though he would have resisted the idea that he had developed anything as coherent as a biographical-philosophical 'project', he lived according to the values he espoused in his thinking. The life and work of few thinkers combine to form a whole as much as Baudrillard's.

This is why the authors of this book do not share our subject's (or object's) own scepticism about biography, and are convinced a critical life of Baudrillard is not only possible but needed. His ideas are hard to understand. But our hope is that by considering both his life and work together readers may be given a fresh insight into Baudrillard's way of thinking. His ideas about virtuality, hyperreality, technology and sexuality, and his provocations about the end of things that defined the modern world – production, human agency, history – have only become more relevant in our age of globalization, data production, digital culture, automation and AI. To quote the rationale behind a recent academic conference on his work: 'Baudrillard may no longer be around to analyse our world. But he has already done so.'[27]

For all his commitment to disappearance – and probably in spite of his best instincts – Baudrillard always seemed to convey an image of cool. Throughout the 1980s, as he became famous outside France and outside the confines of academia, he frequented American art circles and met many thinkers and artists, and he wrote songs for the Japanese singer Megumi Satsu ('Motel Suicide' and 'Lifting Zodiacal'). Although his books could be abstruse and cryptic, they sold in large quantities to non-academics – helped by the covetable small black paperback format his friend Sylvère Lotringer chose for his Semiotext(e) book series 'Foreign Agents'. He wrote many articles for mainstream French newspapers, especially the left-wing daily *Libération*, but also for more upmarket ones like

Le Monde diplomatique – which enabled him to experiment with another means of transmitting his ideas. He rode the 'foamy crest of the wave' of the fascination with French theory in the United States, being embraced there more than any other figure by artistic communities, cinema and, eventually, Internet culture.[28] He did not want to be a star and appeared nonplussed at adulation. But just that once, in a casino near Las Vegas, he decided to go on stage in a sequinned jacket and intone the lyrics of 'Motel Suicide' to an audience of philosophy-rave-goers.

Baudrillard is still a presence in pop culture iconography. In 2013 two academics published a paper that argued Lady Gaga was 'Baudrillard in drag'.[29] In 2019 the American indie rock band Deerhunter released an album that duplicated the title of his last book, *Why Hasn't Everything Already Disappeared?* (2007). That same year, the French writer Alexandre Labruffe promoted his novel *Chroniques d'une station-service* by stating he wished he were Baudrillard and appearing on TV wearing a cap with the slogan 'Back to Baudrillard' emblazoned upon it. The star-studded 2021 Netflix film satire *Don't Look Up* was described as an illustration of what Baudrillard called the 'crime of reality'.[30] Two years later came the publication of an introduction to Baudrillard's philosophy that takes the form of a classic Choose Your Own Adventure game-book.[31]

There is a mini-tradition of advertising that uses imagery of Baudrillard, the theorist lauded for his analyses of late capitalism and consumer society. The graphic designer Jean-Paul Goude photographed advertiser Frédéric Beigbeder reading Baudrillard's *The Consumer Society* in 2008. The luxury fashion brand Gucci featured as part of its Autumn/Winter 2021 campaign a reclining model with *Simulacra and Simulation* open on the floor beside her, next to a riding crop and helmet. There are, inevitably, a number of Internet memes featuring Baudrillard. One features a smoking Baudrillard saying 'Fuck *The Matrix*. I invented that shit.' In 2022 the businessman and investor Elon Musk chose another to accompany a tweet: a close-up of Baudrillard drawing on a cigarette with the words 'looney toons are just normal tunes to me' superimposed upon it.

Despite his careful attempts to disappear, Baudrillard the man (or a version of him), the brilliant, uncompromising thinker and writer, the emblem of the cigarette-toting cool French theorist, is still present today. It is pertinent to reread him now, because of the resonance of his ironic analyses of the contemporary world. In *America* he writes:

> Nothing evokes the end of the world more than a man running straight ahead on a beach, swathed in the sounds of his Walkman, cocooned in the solitary sacrifice of his energy, indifferent even to catastrophes since he expects destruction to come only as the fruit of his own efforts, from exhausting the energy of a body that has in his own eyes become useless.[32]

Throughout the book he is struck by the legions of joggers who course through the 'astral American' cityscapes and concludes that 'this entire society, including its active, productive part – everyone – is running straight ahead, because they have lost the formula for stopping'.[33] This is an example of one of Baudrillard's repeated refrains, that the apparent development of civilization and the human species is inevitably – like all systems – reaching a point where it will implode, reverse itself, destroy itself.

We write nearly four decades after Baudrillard was watching the joggers in California. Some readers may find it hard to argue against his assumption that the human race is committing suicide. The jogger simply expends energy for no reason, simulating production and progress whereas in fact the activity is banal. Other readers may disagree, but are still intrigued by the life and work of the man who asserted it. Of course, like so many of his refrains, this is an exercise in Baudrillardian exaggeration, a piece of black humour which fits with his image as *eiron,* as laughing skull. But still . . . As Susan Sontag once said, 'in time, Baudrillard will increase in significance.'[34] This is one of the core hypotheses that inspired this book.

1

Belonging and Breaking Away, 1929–66

Identity is a dream pathetic in its absurdity.[1]

Looking back on his life, in the early 2000s, Jean Baudrillard observed that

> Few world events are emblematic of a life, and form part of one's biography on the same footing as, and sometimes more profoundly than, personal events. I pride myself on having cut a single swathe from the Wall Street Crash of 1929 to the collapse of the Twin Towers in September 2001.[2]

He was fond of constructing ironic, fragmentary personal histories, and fascinated by major 'symbolic' events, like 9/11. Framing his birth and old age by two such historical moments makes his individuality dissolve into their significance. It is also notable that these remarks do not place his life in a specifically French historical context. Baudrillard liked to proclaim an 'anti-nationalist' or even 'anti-cultural' position. He would always think of himself as 'an internal exile'.[3] Somewhere inside himself, he thought, there was a need to distance himself from his origins, 'from what is closer to the bone, for that which is closer to one's own culture, one's country, family . . . that from which one cannot escape'. At the same time, he maintained that he always attached an importance to 'intimacy, roots, ancestry'.[4]

The most valuable parts of his ancestry were his 'peasant' origins. He discussed these at length in a November 1991 interview:

My grandparents were peasants. My parents became civil servants. A traditional family development which meant that they left the countryside and settled in a town. I was the first member of the tribe, so to speak, to do some studying, that was the point of rupture, when I broke away and got started. Apart from that I don't have much to say. I was not brought up in an intellectual milieu – there was nothing around me – my parents were what they were, not even petit bourgeois, or perhaps very lowly petit bourgeois. It was not a cultural environment.[5]

This sense of who he really was became a powerful part of the armoury he deployed against the intellectual milieu he would inhabit for the major part of his life. He would cite his social origins in order to portray himself as an alien driven into the world of the elite. Rather than being worried he would not fit in, he was determined to stay true to his outsider status: 'I'm instinctively suspicious of everything which is aesthetic or part of culture as a whole. I'm something of a peasant or a barbarian at heart, and I do my best to stay that way.'[6] He called himself an 'untutored amateur', insisting that 'I don't belong to the club, to the seraglio.' He acknowledged there was 'a bit of affectation on my part as far as this [stance] goes, but I am as I am'.[7]

Baudrillard did not get into the École normale supérieure (the elite 'grande école' in Paris). Nor was he successful in his *agrégation* exam (his teaching qualification). But these 'failures' were more about his preference for maintaining the 'outsider observer' position than any academic shortcomings on Baudrillard's part. In fact, he was sure his peasant's roots had equipped him with a more practical value – laziness:

This laziness is, in essence, rural. It is founded on a sentiment of 'natural' merit and equilibrium. One must never do too much. It is a principle of discretion and respect for the equivalence of work and the earth: the peasant gives, but it is up to the earth and to the Gods to give the rest – the essential. A principle of respect for that which does not come from work, and will never come from it . . . I detest buoyant activism in fellow citizens, initiatives, social responsibility, ambition, competition. These are exogenous values, urban, performative, pretentious. They are industrial qualities. Laziness on the other hand, is a natural energy.[8]

Laziness does not seem an obvious feature of the life of someone who published over forty books, wrote innumerable essays and journalistic pieces, gave countless interviews and talks at conferences and events, travelled enthusiastically and produced thousands of photographs. Being idle is really shorthand for his determination to challenge the bourgeois values, the 'initiatives, social responsibility, ambition, competition', that underpinned academic life as much as they did business or industry. It is also perhaps an acknowledgement that he found his work effortless and enjoyable. Baudrillard's wife, Marine, would point out that 'To Jean, it never felt as if he was working.'[9]

Much of Baudrillard's childhood – and to a certain extent, the entire first part of his life until he started a PhD at the age of 34 – lingers in silence. This is no doubt partly because of his taciturn nature. But it is also the result of his deliberate strategy of 'forgetting'. When asked about the literature he would read in his youth, he wondered aloud what he could say other than list examples of novels or novelists (Faulkner, Dostoevsky, Nabokov, Bellow):

> To go deeper one should make an effort to look for one's own traces, but because I did everything I could to erase them, it becomes difficult to exhume them even for myself . . . And on top of that, this obsession – that is almost a perversion – to forget, to erase, to eliminate things, the ones that are the more intimate for me.[10]

He had a habit in interviews of resorting to this obsession when the discussion got closer to personal matters. In fact he would often

Chaumont-Porcien, 1939. In interviews Baudrillard would repeatedly refer to his roots by defining himself as a peasant.

denigrate the very idea of identity: 'Identity is a dream pathetic in its absurdity. You dream of being yourself when you've got nothing better to do. You dream of that when you've lost all singularity (and culture is precisely the extreme form of singularity of a society).'[11] This carefully preserved practice of self-erasure confirms the sense of Baudrillard as an irremediably solitary and independent figure.

Jean Baudrillard was born on 27 July 1929 in Reims. His father was a gendarme and his mother was a postal worker. His childhood and adolescence, from what we can gather, seems harmonious and largely uneventful. He would holiday at his grandparents' house in the small town of Chaumont-Porcien (in the Le Porcien region of northeast France, between Champagne and the Ardennes). One key period – never referred to directly by the mature Baudrillard – is his childhood experience of the Second World War and in particular the occupation of France by German and Italian military forces when the authoritarian Vichy regime was in place. Reims was occupied from July 1940 until the liberation of France in the summer of 1944. The city was also the location of the Allied forces headquarters where the declaration of their eventual victory was signed on 7 May 1945. It is possible Baudrillard may not have remembered much about his experiences. It would be equally understandable if this surely unsettling period was later subject to his practice of studiously forgetting his past. It is notable that the Second World War is not included in the shorthand history of major events which he used to mark the scope of his life.

It has been reported that the young Baudrillard was evacuated from his village on an ox-cart during the French Occupation, though this cannot be corroborated.[12] He certainly attended a school away from his parents, but it is not clear whether this was a boarding school, or, more likely, because he had been sent, like many children in French towns and cities during the war, to the safer environs of his grandparents' home in the countryside about 65 kilometres (40 mi.) north of Reims. The letters the ten-year-old Jean sent back to his parents are full of simple details which provide an insight into the rhythms of French life at the time, albeit under occupation – being in class, going for walks, helping his grandparents – and give the impression of relative stability. They suggest that the young Baudrillard was fond of both his parents and his grandparents. He shared a bed with his grandfather. He remembers his grandad buying a pig for '5 francs per kilo' from a Mr Durtercq and both men killing it and subsequently being sent 'meat, blood sausage'.[13] He reports that they 'made cider yesterday morning, to be refreshed for a fortnight'.[14] He reports that he 'succeeded in finishing the crosswords today from *L'Éclaireur*. I went back to catechism, and I got an A.'[15] One letter from 1939 mentions a soldier, an Adjutant-Major, who sleeps in their house. Another, addressed to his mother, conveys the monotony of his life in wartime:

> Here, it is always the same thing. We always have the same soldiers. The one that stays at home brought his wife, so we have one more resident. She is a pretty woman, very young and really kind, but showy. She eats at home for lunch and in the morning. Our kitchen is now fully installed. There is a soldier that comes in this kitchen every night. He makes me revise my lessons. And looks at my homework. He is a comrade. The weather is always the same, desolate and sad. If it is not raining, it drizzles, and

there is always something that bothers us. Last week was alright, but this week the bad weather never ceases. Even if it is noon, it is still dark. I have nothing else to tell you.[16]

It is most likely that these soldiers, 'comrades', are repatriated French soldiers, but this is never made clear.

When he reports on his progress at school, we can observe the emergence of a competitive academic spirit. He does well in maths, is joint first in the class for catechism (the results are 'posted on the church's door'), receives A grades in all three exams one month, and observes that 'as there are not very good pupils in spelling, I think I may have had the best result.'[17]

After the war, back in Reims, and undertaking his Baccalauréat between 1946 and 1947 at the Collège des Bons-Enfants, life returned to a kind of normality. In an interview later he recalled that he would often go to the local cinema, the Alhambra:

There were some Tarzan films, like 'Aloa, Daughter of the Isles' . . . it was wonderful. I even used to go in secret. (Laughter.) Yes, my father would be at the front of the auditorium and at the end I would slip out quickly so that he couldn't see me. And then there were some Jean Gabin films, '*Quai des Brumes*' . . . and of course I adored Michèle Morgan like everybody else. I was deeply in love with her. *La Symphonie Pastorale*, I must have seen it four or five times in a row. That was the sentimental phase . . . I think it is good to go through a rather hysterical, a rather sentimental period like that.[18]

The teenage Baudrillard performed superbly at the Collège des Bons-Enfants, helped, he later claimed, by a phenomenal memory. He achieved his Baccalauréat in 1947, and won a prize in the 'Concours général' – the most prestigious academic competition in France – for his special ability in German. This enabled his passage into the elite Parisian high school Lycée Henri IV, to take the 'classes préparatoires' which would enable him to sit the entry examination for the École normale supérieure. He worked extremely hard at the

The Alhambra cinema, Reims, 1950s.

Lycée to compensate for the absence of a cultural environment at home: 'That's when an enormous amount of primitive accumulation took place. It was a period in my life when I worked really hard at acquiring an enormous amount.'[19]

However, once at Lycée Henri IV, in the middle of the academic year there came the moment Baudrillard later described as a sudden rupture, 'a break, a violent break, Rimbaud-like if you will, following a forced, very rapid process of assimilation during my adolescent years'.[20] Without warning – at least to his family – the eighteen-year-old suddenly dropped out of the school and in 1948 moved south to Arles, in the Provence region in the south of France, apparently to work as a bricklayer. He writes to his parents, explaining his deeply felt desire to be freed from the average existence they had imagined for him. He asks them to stop helping him by sending him food and money, not to be mad at him, and explains his decision: 'I am not on holiday relying on your money . . . You can be at peace, I am not following Van Gogh's path, even though one would desire to do what he has done.'[21] The painter Vincent van Gogh had made a similar move in 1888 from Paris to Arles (though was much older than Baudrillard when he did so) to benefit from warmer weather and invigorate his work with the bright colours of Provence.

In a subsequent letter Baudrillard says more:

I am not tempted to explain what is happening to me. I left the Lycée Henri IV Sunday 18th. Obviously, it is not because I do not want to work. Life will now be much harder, I know that. I do not rely on you . . . I am simply looking for a bit more heroism than there is in your life, and in the life you planned in all fairness for me. Your kid has finally gone crazy. I'd rather imagine that it is madness, but it is something else. I do not feel ingratitude, do not be mad at me. Here it is too cowardly, Reims is too cowardly. I have lost one trimester asking myself if I could allow myself to do this to you, now I am sure of myself. For a religious vocation, one leaves everything. It is the same without God. I do not regret anything. Be strong enough not to regret anything. Sending you more love than ever.[22]

This letter reveals a boldness and single-mindedness that would characterize Baudrillard's life as an intellectual. In fact it is an early example of a deeper break: the rejection of what he thought of as the classic academic means of progressing, its prescribed ways of thinking and forms of expression, and how to forge a career. He would later insist that if he had followed the expected route to the École normale he would have 'acquired a good solid philosophical culture'.[23] Instead his break ensured that while he was successful academically, and eventually became a philosopher, he was never 'trained' – and this was ultimately a virtue, even though he would always harbour a paradoxical sense of resentment that he was never fully accepted by the French philosophical establishment. The letter also proves how strongly Baudrillard resisted following the paths expected of him. He later acknowledged the departure from Henri IV set the pattern for many of the relationships – with movements and disciplines, and perhaps with people – in his adult life:

breaking away from my parents established a mode of rupture which then by a process of transposition influenced other things. I have always been in a virtual state of rupture: with the university, even with the political world where I was able to get involved but always only at a distance. So there's a kind of prototype in my childhood, adolescence, etc.[24]

It is not clear why he went to Provence, nor exactly what he did there. He mentions a non-religious sense of vocation, but the motivation behind his move to Arles is more mysterious than Van Gogh's. It was not yet, it seems, to take the first steps in becoming a writer or thinker – at least not practically, since he seems not to have produced anything. He did later say, however, that he had written 'other' works before his first publications in the 1950s – not essays, 'but texts difficult to classify, poetic texts, if I may use that term', but had burned most of them.[25] Perhaps his deliberate choice not to live on his wits, working as, say, a teacher (that would come a few years later), was a way of reconnecting with his peasant origins. It certainly seems significant that he should reference Rimbaud and Van Gogh – two innovative, expressive artists – in describing his sudden flight from Henri IV. The fierce independence and rejection of bourgeois social norms which would define his intellectual career means Baudrillard could be regarded as a late-twentieth-century equivalent of the rebellious, solitary modernist artist. In any case, it seems that the move to Arles in the late 1940s was more likely the beginning of a period travelling around France, paying his way by working at menial jobs, becoming part of the itinerant workforce required throughout the post-war reconstruction of the nation.[26]

By 1949 he was back in Paris, studying German at the Sorbonne, the University of Paris, France's leading university. He chose German because it was clear he had a special talent for the language, though later he would state – perhaps tongue-in-cheek, playing up to his image as untutored philosophical amateur – that this was the lazy option, preferable to selecting philosophy.[27] In any case, the value of his university study paled in comparison to one strand of extracurricular education he could pursue now he was back in Paris: his immersion in 'pataphysics'.

Commonly summarized as 'the science of imaginary solutions',[28] pataphysics was an absurdist pseudo-philosophy devised by the avant-garde writer Alfred Jarry at the end of the nineteenth century.[29] It had a special connection to Reims, as this was the city of the legendary *Le Grand Jeu*, a Surrealist magazine founded by René Daumal, Roger Gilbert-Lecomte and Roger Vailland in 1928, just before Baudrillard's birth. All three had in fact attended the same school as he did, the Collège des Bons-Enfants in Reims. They intended *Le Grand Jeu* to 'mak[e] men despair of themselves and society'.[30] Though the magazine was short-lived (lasting only until 1930) the group's air of decadent experimentalism hung over the city for years, and was breathed in by the young Jean Baudrillard.[31] His philosophy teacher at the Collège des Bons-Enfants was Emmanuel Peillet, one of the founders of the Collège de pataphysique in 1948, an ironic administrative centre for the study of pataphysics based in Paris – or, as it styled itself, a 'society of scholarly and useless research'. Baudrillard was introduced to pataphysics by Peillet, and during his time at the Sorbonne he became a member of the Collège.

Baudrillard's first essay worthy of publication was titled 'Pataphysics' and completed in 1952, though it remained unpublished until 2005. This piece, and a draft essay on 'Ubu' he had worked on a couple of years earlier,[32] were written because he felt pulled towards two extremes: Jarry's character Ubu Roi (a corpulent portrait in stupidity who nevertheless embodies a pataphysical impulse to expose the frailty of everything) and Artaud, in whose primitivism he saw a model for the rejection of the modern culture of 'production' (as he would later describe it). In a radio interview in 1988 Baudrillard confessed to being one of the writers, affiliated to the Collège de pataphysique, of a fake long poem purportedly written by Rimbaud – capitalizing on the long-rumoured existence of the poet's lost masterpiece, *La Chasse spirituelle* – which was unveiled to the public by the writer Pascal Pia in May 1949. By July 1949 it had been exposed as a forgery by André Breton.[33]

Its oppositional, parodic spirit means pataphysics cannot be defined in the way one can normally define an artistic movement, far less a science. Scientific method concentrates on drawing general rules and principles from the analysis of a particular object

Emmanuel Peillet, Baudrillard's philosophy teacher at school, and co-founder of the Collège de pataphysique.

or objects. Pataphysics concentrates on exceptions, that which is singular or individual, in order to confound the system. It is better understood as a spirit which can be found in the work of a range of avant-garde artists from the Surrealists through Marcel Duchamp to the Marx Brothers, as well as in what the Collège de pataphysique called 'patacessors' – those who helped develop the science unwittingly. Baudrillard's own 1952 definition of pataphysics is 'philosophy of the gaseous state'. The gaseous is the realm in which nothing is solid; 'all phenomena are absolutely gaseous.'[34]

His pataphysical instincts remained throughout his life, and help explain the provocative interventions he would make as a writer or commentator. His book *Forget Foucault* (1977) is a good example. In 2001 he remarked that 'Pataphysics remains a game, and at the same time a violent ferment.'[35] In particular, the pataphysical spirit of 'reversibility' became central to Baudrillard's thought. Though reversibility is a concept explored by many previous philosophers (from Heraclitus to Nietzsche), in a pataphysical context it refers to the possibility, or likelihood – even an unavoidable destiny – that every system will weaken itself by virtue of its own operations and go into 'reverse'.

The young Baudrillard's growing self-identification in pataphysics undoubtedly fulfilled his craving for rupture and, specifically, contributed to his abrupt departure from Henri IV. As he later said, 'making the *sacrificio dell intelletto* – that was the impact of pataphysics on my existence'.[36] It also connected – however improbably – with his 'peasant' urge to puncture the flatulent and conformist pretensions of official knowledge and academia:

They say that stupidity is a crime, but it seems to me that explanation is the real crime. I understand very well when things are explained to me, but deep down, I am at one with those who will never understand. A brute slumbers within me who sneers at such understanding and doesn't give a damn for intelligence. With those who understand, I make a contract of intelligence, but with the others, at the very same instant, I secretly make a pact of stupidity. The intellectual or the person who claims the title (there are no others) is the one who has broken that pact of stupidity, and feels released from it. In doing so, he plumbs the very depths of stupidity.[37]

Baudrillard's flirtation with the 'official' pataphysical movement in France fits a pattern that was to play out repeatedly whenever it came to engaging with collectives throughout his life. The 1952 essay confirmed his involvement with the Collège de pataphysique, but also marked the end of it. His discomfort with the institutionalization of pataphysics is one reason why the piece remained unpublished for over five decades – though he also said later that its topic was somehow too personal for it to appear, and he had quickly decided to move on 'to other things'.[38] He felt that 'the pataphysical entourage was adopting the same conformism, the same institutional infatuation that Ubu himself had.'[39] Baudrillard was always acutely aware that the trap of reversibility opens up whenever a group challenges an orthodoxy. In doing so it risks installing itself as the mirror of that which it has challenged, both in terms of its authoritative intellectual position and its internal hierarchies.

Throughout the 1950s Baudrillard preferred to read poetry rather than philosophy, immersing himself not just in Artaud but in Rimbaud, Hölderlin and Pierre Klossowski.[40] In this period Baudrillard also wrote a seventeen-poem sequence – as part of some of the early writing he chose not to destroy – entitled *Stucco Angel*, which was eventually published as a separate volume in 1978.[41] It is tempting to read Baudrillard the philosopher 'backwards' through this text, especially when it features phrases that now sound distinctively 'Baudrillardian', such as 'everything is reversible' or 'the game of opposite thoughts'. Baudrillard's essay 'The Orders of Simulacra', originally published in *Symbolic Exchange and Death* (1976), contains a section entitled 'Stucco Angel', which examines the capacity of stucco in the Renaissance period to 'imitate everything – velvet curtains, wooden corniches, charnel swelling of the flesh'.[42] The early poem is about the gap between image and reality – embodied by the figure of the stucco angel, a plaster-rendering of the kind which recurs in classical and baroque art – and trades in what would become familiar Baudrillardian themes: language, femininity, sexuality, death. The fact that it eventually surfaced between the publication of his books *Symbolic Exchange and Death* and *Seduction* (1979), which deal with similar themes, suggests a connection between Baudrillard's early and later perception of the world.

But rather than exploring in poetry the kind of topics Baudrillard would meditate in his later writing, *Stucco Angel* should be read as a sequence of lyrical poems that use desire as a way of meditating the fleeting nature of perception and thought. Its use of natural imagery suggests the influence of the Romantic poet-philosopher Friedrich Hölderlin, and its refraction of external reality through subjective consciousness recalls German expressionist poetry of the late nineteenth and early twentieth centuries. The world outside, never described directly but metonymically (fields, grass, the forest, halls, a flower market), is transfigured by the poet's state of mind. It is impossible to grasp exactly what is happening, where it takes place or who the speaker is. However, it is preoccupied with the real and the imaginary of erotic love. The eponymous angel is either the focal point for the desire the speaker feels for a real woman he once knew or who is at times with him, or stands in for a real woman:

A bird, is she or
deer dress
or clover smoke
or doll of medlar fruit
it is her
unlyrical and surreptitious
less far and brief, but far
as if it were yesterday
it is her of whom
I would never have had the idea
on my own.[43]

Baudrillard clearly had a gift for poetry. Even though *Stucco Angel* appears to be his only work of poetry (at least that we are aware of), it displays a talent for triggering ideas in the mind of the reader through elliptical, economical and metaphorical fragments of language rather than a systematic development of a theme, and in this it resembles the experience of reading his later prose writing.

In 1952 Baudrillard was on the move again. He obtained his first career job teaching in Tübingen, a university city in southwest Germany, and also worked at translating Hölderlin. In 1956 he was back in France, and for the next decade, until 1966, taught German literature and philosophy in lycées in Paris. In 1957–8 he undertook his military service at the Satory military centre south of Versailles, just outside Paris. In this period he married his first wife, Lucile, and had two children, Gilles and Anne, born in 1952 and 1953 respectively. He and Lucile separated in 1965. Baudrillard almost never spoke about his children publicly, and said virtually nothing about fatherhood. In a 1989 interview he was asked directly: 'Do you have children? Do they make you feel optimistic?' His response was oddly factual and emotionless: 'I had two. Today they are grown-up. Perhaps I was a bad father because I didn't project my own personal hopes on to them, so they were carried along by their own impetus. They do their own thing.'[44] He does not take the interviewer's bait about the value of parenthood, and focuses on his children's independence and that which comes from his own position of father. There is no hint of any special relationship.

Baudrillard's immersion in German culture for over a decade in the 1950s and '60s may seem hard to square with the fact that he eventually became so firmly established in radical French thought (albeit maintaining his position on the margins). Part of its value was precisely because he did not consider his engagement with German literature and philosophy a formal training, as it would have been if he had studied German 'systematically' at the École normale supérieure.[45] It would give him the opportunity later to short-circuit any inflated praise – and any suspicion that he was a privileged 'insider' – by claiming he was merely an insignificant Professor of German. 'Je ne suis qu'un petit prof d'allemand,' he would say.[46] As well as fuel to kindle his outsider identity, studying German and Germany enabled him to explore many of his interests by approaching them from fresh perspectives. He read philosophers like Schopenhauer or Nietzsche and writers like Hölderlin and Brecht on his own terms (rather than as part of a prescribed programme), as well as encountering soon-to-be-influential sociological and cultural texts not yet available in French translation, such as the Frankfurt School's critiques of contemporary culture.[47]

Baudrillard's interest in German language and culture was the platform for his early career as a cultural critic. In 1962 and 1963 he contributed articles on literature – such as reviews of books by William Styron and Italo Calvino – to *Les Temps modernes*, one of the most influential post-war French journals of the cultural left. Most interesting of these for any consideration of the writer Baudrillard himself was to become is perhaps his essay on Uwe Johnson, the avant-garde East German novelist. He notes Johnson's ability to convey how specific objects confound the efforts of the subject to control them, such as 'talking' cigarette-vending machines or the eiderdown which tends to slip off the bed during the night.[48] Baudrillard contributed the accompanying text to René Burri's classic 1963 work of documentary photography, *Les Allemands* – a counterpart to Robert Frank's *Les Américains* – compiling it almost completely from quotations (showing an early liking for fragmentary, impressionistic prose) which highlighted the contrast between the two sides of the divided Germany, East and West, and the process of reconstructing West Germany.[49]

Germany – a nation coming to terms with how to regenerate itself after the war – was a powerful example of how political power and modernization manifested in the lives of the people who lived through it. Baudrillard's interest in German culture both differed from and complemented his fascination with pataphysics and avant-garde art. He was commissioned to translate into French a number of German political texts. These included, in 1963, Bertolt Brecht's *Dialogue d'exilés* (Refugee Conversations). Brecht would always be important for Baudrillard, and especially this book of satirical dialogues. Baudrillard was particularly fond of a remark by the character Kalle: 'Where nothing is in its place, there's disorder. Where everything is in its place there's nothing there, and that's order.'[50] This line embodies what would come to be the quintessential 'Baudrillardian' logic: 'order' equals reality, which is mere simulation.

He also translated a number of works by the German artist and writer Peter Weiss, including his most celebrated piece, *Marat/Sade* (1965), and his *Discourse on Vietnam* (1968), which had been another influence behind Baudrillard's intertextual method in *Les Allemands*. Through Weiss he became associated with the Gruppe 47 collective, an informal association of German-speaking writers which also included Hans Werner Richter, Alfred Andersch, Günter Grass and Heinrich Böll. Gruppe 47 was dedicated to rescuing contemporary German writing from the damage done to the reputation of the German language and culture by the war. To Baudrillard the group's mission was a cog in a larger mechanism, the collective German confrontation of 'a fundamental problem: how to erase their war-guilt, their total defeat'.[51]

The idea of Germany as a specific example of a broader contemporary problem never left Baudrillard. In 1989, the year the Cold War ended, he wrote that the now-crumbling Berlin Wall represented 'frozen history', a world in which nothing more, no events, could happen. The wall itself was a symbol of a static relation between the two systems, capitalism and communism.[52] Returning there as the wall was being dismantled, he was struck by the fact he had been there at the start (the wall was built in 1961) and at the end; it was as if he had observed the whole cycle.

Baudrillard's literary reviews appear outdated now, rather pedestrian in comparison to the enigmatic verve of his later writing, and even to his 1952 essay on pataphysics. It is strange to read a Baudrillard who praises Calvino's 'sincerity' and criticizes his 'irresolution', when his later self would probably have been suspicious of the former attitude and promoted the latter one as seductive. But his early analyses of literature were clearly a formative exercise in writing about society and culture. He was never destined to become a literary critic, and never planned to be. But his early literary sensibility shaped his philosophy:

> If I started anywhere it was with poetical things, Rimbaud, Artaud, etc., Nietzsche, Bataille. It was things like that, they were

Henri Lefebvre, 1971.

classical things, not very original, but they were not philosophy. In fact, I've always had a great deal of mistrust for philosophers, so I've developed a kind of allergy which makes me dislike the stereotyped language used in philosophy. Even its most beautiful texts fail to impress me.[53]

Just as significant as his early writings and translations is the fact that in 1963 Baudrillard began a *thèse de troisième cycle* (doctoral work) at the Sorbonne. He chose to undertake this in sociology rather than German, apparently at the suggestion of his supervisor, Henri Lefebvre, a renowned Marxist philosopher and sociologist. Both the change of direction and working with Lefebvre paved the way for his entrance into an exalted Parisian intellectual milieu, which he initially took part in enthusiastically, though warily. In 1962 he briefly joined the psychoanalytic thinker Félix Guattari in founding a radical left-wing – and short-lived – Franco-Chinese Maoist association which published a newspaper. Along with Lucile (and a great many doyens of French theory at the time) he attended the famous literary theorist Roland Barthes' seminar series on rhetoric at the École pratique des hautes études between 1964 and 1969. In the 1960s he also crossed paths with the polymath intellectual Edgar Morin and the experimental novelist Georges Perec.

In September 1966 Baudrillard took up a teaching post in sociology at the new University of Nanterre in Paris. After much wandering, both literal and metaphorical, his trajectory from talented 'untutored' outsider to globally renowned thinker begins here, at this point. Establishing himself as an academic and mingling with the Parisian intelligentsia meant that, in one way, he had finally arrived somewhere stable and belonged to something enduring, yet in a position where he could perform his self-constructed role as peasant outsider. He would continue to seek ways to remain outside and to reject the world he had entered. The discipline of sociology (a subject with no *agrégation*, the competitive civil service qualification) was a marginal academic subject at the time, and Nanterre a radical and oppositional institution, too. Both suited Baudrillard perfectly, at least to begin with.

2

Objects and Objections, 1966–70

The first obsession I remember is an obsession with the object.[1]

In the summer of 1966, at Nanterre, Baudrillard defended his
doctoral dissertation. His thesis was entitled 'The System of Objects'
and he was examined by a prestigious panel comprising Henri
Lefebvre, Roland Barthes and Pierre Bourdieu. All three figures were
highly respected in France, but at the time were also swept up in the
beginnings of what would become a wave of international academic
fascination with French theory, which would not subside for nearly
four decades.

French theory is close to philosophical thought, but more literary
and speculative in spirit, and more interdisciplinary in method.
It was influenced by theories of language, semiology, Marxism
and psychoanalysis, and was geared up to providing a critique of
contemporary society and culture, usually from a broadly left-wing
perspective. It found a devoted readership in the United States in
the 1960s and '70s because of the intermeshing of academic fashion,
artistic trends and the counter-cultural impulse at that time. Barthes
and Bourdieu – as well as other prominent names such as Jacques
Derrida, Michel Foucault, Jacques Lacan, Louis Althusser, Julia
Kristeva and Jean-François Lyotard – 'took on an aura that up to
then had been reserved only for the heroes of American mythology
or the celebrities of "show business"'.[2]

Ironically, in France many of these figures were considered
marginal to specific disciplines, or treated as distinct individual
thinkers rather than as members of any movement. But in the

Baudrillard as a young academic, beginning his career as a lecturer in sociology at Nanterre.

United States, and latterly in the United Kingdom and Australia, French theory became a 'brand', linking together under broad umbrella terms such as 'poststructuralism' or 'postmodernism' a range of theorists who otherwise were quite different from each other.[3] In a few years Baudrillard himself would be enlisted as a member, and in fact, during French theory's high point in the 1990s, he would become arguably the brand's most celebrated and representative figure. But in 1966 it would have been hard to pick three more pre-eminent doctoral panellists in the general area of cultural sociology. Each one, in different ways, exerted a significant influence on Baudrillard's early career.

His thesis passed, despite Bourdieu's misgivings about his approach. Bourdieu remarked that 'this thesis is to sociology what golden is to apple: it is shiny, but it is not sociology.'[4] As marginal and fluid a discipline as sociology was in French universities, Baudrillard would face similar scepticism about his credentials as a 'true sociologist' many times in the years to come, and it never worried him. Looking back at his early career at Nanterre in 1999, he said:

> I started instead from semiology, psychoanalysis, Marxism . . . intellectual trends that, in a way, were not disciplinary, at least not at the time. I was not a sociologist; I became one when I arrived at Nanterre. I became one after the students, since I was just a week ahead of them when I prepared my courses. Sociology has never been a kind of territory for me. And even less as a research activity. Rather, my first impulse was to 'get through it' . . . I worked with Bourdieu without entering into the same considerations.[5]

Roland Barthes, the other external member of the jury, would have appreciated Baudrillard's thesis more. Its analysis had a strongly Barthesian flavour. Its title recalled Barthes' book *The System of Fashion* (published in 1967 but written between 1957 and 1963) and some of its ideas had taken root as contributions to Barthes' seminar in the mid-1960s.[6] Baudrillard would later say that reading Barthes' seminal work of cultural analysis, *Mythologies* (1957), was 'really an event . . . a love at first sight, another reading of the world'.[7] Interviewed by the radio programme *France Culture* in 2000, he reiterated his view that for him Barthes had never been 'a mentor, just a master'.[8] By contrast, even though he liked Lefebvre and felt they worked well together, he found some of his intellectual positions naive, 'too set', too redolent of 'old France'.[9] There was an undoubtedly Oedipal dimension to their relationship, given the influence Lefebvre had had on Baudrillard's career. 'He thought I was a disciple and this in the end spoilt our relationship because I was not his disciple.'[10]

As Nanterre sociologists, Lefebvre and Baudrillard were soon both caught up in one of the most dramatic social crises in modern French history: the rebellious *évènements* of May 1968, which nearly brought down the French government. The University of Nanterre was intended, when founded in 1964, as an annex of the Sorbonne, and its spirit was initially one of excitement and optimism as the new university was keen to demonstrate its autonomy. This, alongside its novelty and its location to the west of Paris in what was then an urban wasteland, gave Nanterre the air of the 'wild west'. It was an ideal place for an internal-outsider like Baudrillard. But its outlier feel also seemed to make it ideally suited for expressions of political unrest.[11] A student protest about gender discrimination in the women's halls of residence took place on 21 March 1967, and although it was ended peacefully by police, this led to the formation soon after of the radical activist group the Enragés de Nanterre. A year later, on 20 March 1968, an occupation of a university building by 142 students to express solidarity with a Nanterre student, Xavier Langlade, who had been arrested after taking part in an 'anti-imperialist' protest in central Paris, also ended peacefully after a few hours. However, the university's reaction to this later event was heavy-handed. It defined the student actions as 'terrorist', proposed a university-based police force, and closed the university temporarily to prevent further uprisings. A larger activist organization, Mouvement du 22 Mars, was formed.[12]

These events cemented the university's reputation as 'Nanterre la rouge'. The university was shut down again on 2 May 1968 after another anti-imperialist protest. Aggrieved students decided to gather at the Sorbonne in central Paris on 3 May, where they were joined by hundreds of others. Further arrests and crackdowns inevitably ensued, leading to the temporary closure of the Sorbonne. Subsequent demonstrations in the days after led to the infamous 'Night of the Barricades' on 10–11 May, when as many as 20,000 people joined in protests throughout the Latin Quarter, uprooting trees, street signs and cobblestones to create barriers. Around 500 students were arrested and hundreds of people were hospitalized, including more than 250 police officers. These events triggered the largest concentration of industrial action in European history, a seven-week protest involving around 10 million striking workers. By the end of May France was on the brink of armed civil war.

Students in a corridor at Nanterre University, April 1968.

The worst was avoided when President Charles de Gaulle returned from hiding in West Germany and dissolved the National Assembly, promising new elections, wage increases and social reforms. Eventually he was elected with a massive majority. By the end of the year, crisis averted, the decision was made to reduce student overcrowding in Paris by dividing the Sorbonne into thirteen smaller universities.

No one could argue that the *évènements* were triggered directly by the writings of the new generation of French theorists. Nor were the protests unified in terms of their political motivations, as they were fuelled by a range of anti-authoritarian perspectives, from communism to libertarianism, and the specific grievances ranged from local student concerns to broader anti-Vietnam, anti-imperialist and decolonial impulses.[13] But theory was certainly in tune with much of the oppositional sentiment. At their heart was a topic central to Lefebvre's work, and indeed sociology at Nanterre, at the time: the politicized contents and conditions of 'everyday life'. Lefebvre's article 'The Right to the City' – its title effectively a slogan which captured the feeling behind the protests – was published the same year as the uprisings.[14] Bourdieu's 1964 book *The Inheritors: French Students and Their Relations to Culture* had also been an inspiration to many involved.

One of the most influential texts was a 1967 book which, like its author, occupied a space on the fringes of French theory, Guy Debord's *The Society of the Spectacle*. Debord was the leader of the collective of anti-authoritarian, avant-garde artists, theorists and political activists known as the Situationist International (or SI). The group were not Marxists exactly, though their commitment to inspiring revolution against the capitalist order ensured an alliance with workers, workers' unions and students. At the heart of their philosophy – as set out in *The Society of the Spectacle* – was the conviction that capitalism deploys a continual stream of detached images that represent people and things and thereby alienate people from real life. Since there was no position outside the spectacle, challenging it had to involve a critique from within, and so the Situationists indulged in staged disruptions such as infiltrating

Students on the Boulevard Saint-Michel, Paris, 3 May 1968, demonstrating against the temporary closure of the Sorbonne.

religious or political ceremonies, or activities that resembled conceptual art, such as producing posters and examples of 'détournement' where adverts or political messaging were hijacked and repurposed.

Baudrillard's attitude to the Situationists was ambivalent. He knew Raoul Vaneigem, a member of the Situationists who had published his own book *The Revolution of Everyday Life* in 1967. Debord was Baudrillard's near-exact contemporary (having been born in 1931), and, like him, another intellectual who instinctively resisted the pull of academia. His theory of the spectacle complemented Baudrillard's own views about media and the image-object, and Baudrillard would often refer to 'the spectacle' in his writing in the years to come. Yet the two never met.[15] This may or may not have been because of Debord's volatile personality.[16] But it was also no doubt because of Baudrillard's mixed feelings about Debord's theory and SI more generally. He accepted Debord's broad definition of the society of the spectacle, but rejected its Marxist theoretical foundations, which he considered far too 'normative'.

As Baudrillard's first two books, *The System of Objects* and *The Consumer Society*, show, he thought a more advanced theory of how signs operate in the modern world was needed – to understand images not as travesties of reality but as reality themselves. There was also the fact that SI believed in aggressive political action. Baudrillard never could. His preferred form of agitation was theory, or what he would later call 'theoretical violence', rather than anything more direct.[17]

Baudrillard was one of the sociologists, along with Lefebvre, who signed a 1967 statement in support of one of the most controversial Situationist pamphlets, 'On the Poverty of Student Life' (which happened to include a criticism of Barthes and Bourdieu, among others), which had led to a scandal at the University of Strasbourg, the expulsion of a group of left-wing students and the closure of the students' union in late 1966.[18] In turn, SI, ever uncompromising, published a document responding to the furore, entitled 'Our Goals and Methods in the Strasbourg Scandal', which mocked the 'Maoist Baudrillard' for his role in 'that wheedling attempt at approval circulated in February by a few decrepit modernist-institutionalists gnawing their meagre bones at the professorial chairs of "Social Sciences" at Nanterre'.[19]

Nevertheless Baudrillard sympathized with the Situationists' anti-authoritarian impulses, appreciated their fusion of artistic practice and politics, and enjoyed their Hegelian strategy of 'immanent critique' and attacking from within. There would remain something fundamentally 'situationist' about Baudrillard's work as it would develop – and self-consciously so. Decades later, surveying ironically the different intellectual identities he had inhabited throughout his life, he described himself as 'pataphysician at twenty – situationist at thirty – utopian at forty – viral and metaleptic at sixty'.[20] Just as the spirit of pataphysics remains detectable throughout his later work, so many of his analyses – such as his description of the Centre Pompidou in 1981 as 'this carcass of flux and signs',[21] or his essay proclaiming that 'The Gulf War Did Not Take Place', a title which resembles a Situationist slogan – might be seen as constructed 'situations'. The characterization of Baudrillard in the 1980s and '90s as an 'intellectual terrorist' (admittedly a label he was happy to adopt himself) echoed the criticisms of the Situationists in the late 1960s.[22]

As with other events in Baudrillard's life it is difficult to separate the reality from the rumour when it comes to his involvement in the events of 1968. There are unverifiable and contradictory accounts that state he either expressed solidarity with the student agitators, took part personally in the demonstrations or was actually in Australia in May of that year, presumably giving a lecture or speaking at a conference.[23] It was likely that his stance was the detached, ironic, almost 'dandified' position he would tend to adopt outwardly in relation to newsworthy events. But on this particular issue, such detachment would not place him at odds with his academic contemporaries. Keeping a distance from the rebellion was the option chosen by most of the prominent French intellectuals at the time, even those whose writings were linked to the events. Bourdieu, for example, was reportedly marking student exam papers as normal in the cafés during the rebellion.[24]

Yet the combination of feverish excitement, the unfulfilled promise of utopia, the reaction of the ruling system and the hysterical way the media amplified the issues surrounding the protests left a deep impression on Baudrillard – one that Sylvère Lotringer would later liken to the effect of the 9/11 terrorist attacks in New York in 2001. Both were 'radical events' in Baudrillard's thinking, extraordinary moments when signs coalesce around a single meaning. As he would later conclude about 9/11, Baudrillard felt that, despite the material gains achieved by workers following the protests, May '68 was far more meaningful in its 'disappearance' than in actuality – it carried a symbolic significance which caused any lasting real consequences to fade.[25]

Specific Baudrillard texts were not cited as influences by those involved in the events of May '68, even though his first book *The System of Objects*, a revision of his doctoral thesis, had been published on 1 January that year. By then, however, he was associated with the Utopie group, a loose collective of Parisian architects, sociologists and urbanists, founded in 1966 at Lefebvre's holiday home in Navarrenx in the Pyrenees. Other members included Hubert Tonka (like Baudrillard, a former assistant of Lefebvre's), fellow sociologists Catherine Cot and René Lourau, and the architects Jean Aubert, Antoine Stinco and Isabelle Auricoste. Utopie's aims were to provide a radical theoretical alternative to professional urban-planning journals, and, more specifically, to counter the De Gaulle government's programme of replanning and expanding Paris in the late 1960s. Many members were influenced by Debord and the Situationists, and the group was an academic arm of the broad oppositional-theory movement whose physical counterpart was the student protests of 1968. The title 'Utopie' was ironic, of course. The group acknowledged that utopia existed only as the 'non-place' of politics, that which is 'never spoken, never on the agenda, always repressed' in politics, history and logic.[26] In an early edition of the journal the group published (also called *Utopie*) an editorial statement, ascribed to the collective, made use of an analogy Baudrillard would later use with Lewis Carroll's Cheshire Cat: utopia resembles 'this smile which floats in the air before the cat appears, and for some time after it has disappeared'.[27] In later Baudrillardian terms, utopia was envisaged as a version of that realm of the real (related to seduction or art) which is made to disappear as a result of the operation of systems.

In 1967 the 37-year-old Baudrillard had begun writing for *Utopie*. Buoyed by the imminent publication of *The System of Objects*, he contributed some of the finest essays in the journal over a period of just over a decade, until 1978, covering a wide range of topics: Marxist theory, terrorism, advertising and the media. In his writings for *Utopie* key Baudrillardian phrases such as the 'mirror of production' and 'the silent majority' first surface, and they were also the platform for a critical engagement with thinkers such as Marshall McLuhan whose ideas related to Baudrillard's developing theories of the media.

The System of Objects was timely in its contribution to the sociology of everyday life. It was part of a surge of interest in objects, technology and consumer society found in the writings of many French thinkers and writers of the 1960s, who focused on objects

Roland Barthes, *c.* 1975.

from a new perspective – considered in terms of consumption rather than production. Prominent examples include Barthes' *Mythologies*, then at the height of its influence, and Georges Perec's novel about listless desire for a consumerist 'good life', *Things: A Story of the Sixties* (1964). Baudrillard's ability in *The System of Objects*, and in his second book, *The Consumer Society* (1970), to combine sociology and cultural analysis to describe the effects of mass-mediated, consumer society, as well as feature eclectic discussions about cars or robots and chapter titles like 'Pax Washing Powder' and 'The Logic of Father Christmas', struck readers as reminiscent of Barthes.[28] Like *Mythologies*, *The System of Objects* conformed to a general Marxist understanding of objects in capitalism as entities whose significance goes far beyond any 'use-value'. It contends that objects must be understood as related to each other, as a system and a syntax, denoting a world that is more complex than it seems: a world of signs.

Baudrillard's particular way of focusing on the object, however, departed from the more conventional sociological interest in the role of the object in social interactions. He was more concerned with the object *itself*. For him – and this would be an enduring concern throughout his work – the object allows us to choose a path away from the question of the subject (or the human being as a component of a social system) which always tended to be privileged in contemporary philosophy:

> The first obsession I remember is an obsession with the object, but understood in a somewhat magical sense. Behind the critique of objects, and of the system of objects, of the consumer society, there was the magic of the object – in this case, an ideal object. At any rate, a clear desire to sweep away the whole culture based on the philosophical subject.[29]

This obsession is apparent everywhere throughout *The System of Objects*. The book meditates the miraculous way the object is inserted into a system of representations and beliefs. From the outset, the proliferation of objects in contemporary society is defamiliarized. 'Could we classify the luxuriant growth of objects as we do a flora or fauna, complete with tropical and glacial species, sudden mutations, and varieties threatened by extinction?', he asks.[30]

In exploring the semiotic grammar of objects, the book's ambition is almost encyclopaedic, and includes pages of analysis of the language of particular objects such as storage structures, lights and lamps, mirrors, clocks, chairs, car parts, lighters and gadgets. Baudrillard considers the materials objects are made from: 'Wood draws its substance from the earth, it lives and breathes and "labours". It has its latent warmth; it does not merely reflect, like glass, but burns from within.'[31] He shows how objects distil concepts such as space and time into tangible, consumable form: just as the car 'eats up miles' (space), so the wristwatch 'eats up time', turning time into 'an object to be consumed'.[32] The impression overall is of the need to restore a sense of mystery about the things we share our world with and normally take for granted: 'Objectively, substances are simply what they are: there is no such thing as a true or a false, a natural or an artificial substance. How could concrete be somehow less "authentic" than stone?'[33]

The System of Objects also considers the special role advertising plays in 1960s society, as a dimension of the system of objects. In readings of contemporary advertisements for brands like Omo or Frigidaire, he demonstrates that advertising is a 'useless and

Las Vegas, photograph by Baudrillard (1996). 'You have only to see Las Vegas, sublime Las Vegas, rise from the desert in its entirety at nightfall bathed in phosphorescent lights, and return to the desert when the sun rises . . . to understand the secret of the desert and the signs to be found there' (*America*, pp. 126–7).

inessential' speech. It is pure 'connotation', having nothing to do with the brands themselves (which are simply 'alibis'), nothing to do with the production or function or value of the objects it promotes (or denotes), but everything to do with legitimating the new form of consumer society. This does not mean that advertising is unimportant; in fact, advertising enables the entire system of consumption to work smoothly. Whether or not we are persuaded by an advertisement for a particular product or brand, participating in the 'discourse on objects' which advertising sustains means we really consume a self-fulfilling story about our own society itself, 'the luxury of a society that projects itself as an agency for dispensing goods and "transcends itself" in a culture'.[34]

After 1968, the University of Nanterre settled into a period of uneasy stability. Efforts had been made to assuage the students and faculty by reorganizing academic units and increasing student involvement in elements of university decision-making such as academic appointments, the curriculum and the budget. But there remained the simmering potential for further political protest. In February 1969 there were reports of a 1,500-strong student strike following accusations that police had infiltrated the Nanterre campus disguised as janitors. 'Approximately half the faculty soon joined in the strike – with sociology and anthropology characteristically taking the lead.'[35] Baudrillard's colleague Jacques Donzelot, who jointly taught the sociology course with him at the end of the 1960s and early 1970s (Donzelot covering the 'birth' bits, like sexuality, the social and politics; Baudrillard the 'deaths' of these things), remembers that the threat of unemployment among academics was constant.[36] Baudrillard, who was promoted from assistant to *maître-assistant* in 1970, was actively involved in defending sociology at Nanterre. He appreciated the platform *Utopie* gave him and his colleagues to do this. The 1968 rebellion now appeared only to have been a transitional moment where the shaking up of the disciplinary frontiers had merely led to them returning to what they were before.

Baudrillard's second book, *The Consumer Society: Myths and Structures*, was commissioned by Éditions Denoël and published in 1970. It is still perhaps Baudrillard's most famous work, though *Simulations* (1983) is a close rival. *The Consumer Society* is still a fixture on university sociology courses, taking its place alongside other essential studies of consumerism by Marcel Mauss, Georges Bataille or Marshall Sahlins. Some of its references to consumer products have inevitably dated, but as one later sociologist proclaimed, 'the book reads as well today as it must have in 1970'; the appeal of *The Consumer Society* is not confined to France: 'it reads at least as well from the context of American society.'[37] In some ways Baudrillard's early books are very unlike the work he would become more generally famous for, which does not sit neatly in any one academic discipline. Yet if he had never written anything else after *The Consumer Society*, this book's contribution to sociology would guarantee Baudrillard's continuing relevance.

The book follows on from the ideas in *The System of Objects* about the 'discourse' of the object and the importance to this discourse of advertising. Baudrillard observes that we have come to live 'not so much alongside other human beings . . . as beneath the mute gaze of mesmerizing, obedient objects which endlessly repeat the same refrain: that of our dumbfounded power, our virtual affluence, our absence one from another'.[38] Consumerism makes this situation into a language, a kind of Barthesian 'myth', a story we tell ourselves about who we are: 'Our society thinks itself and speaks itself as a consumer society. As much as it consumes anything, it consumes *itself* as consumer society, as *idea*. Advertising is the triumphal paean to that idea.'[39]

The book describes the symbolic processes that define this society, which take place in the malls and supermarkets, the 'festive' dimension it attaches to consumption, and its link – though Baudrillard does not mention Debord by name – with the society of the spectacle. Society is held together by the sheer abundance of consumer goods, a multiplication of objects surging through the world, which seemingly offer themselves to us, demanding our adoration. Baudrillard surveys this world:

Profusion, piling high are clearly the most striking descriptive features. The big department stores, with their abundance of canned foods and clothing, of foodstuffs and ready-made garments, are like the primal landscape, the geometrical locus of abundance. But every street, with its cluttered, glittering shop-windows (the least scarce commodity here being light, without which the merchandise would be merely what it is), their displays of cooked meats, and indeed the entire alimentary and vestimentary feast, all stimulate magical salivation.[40]

This luxurious spectacle conveys more than the fact that there is a breathtakingly vast quantity of goods. It impresses on us the 'presence of surplus' and the fact that this surplus magically negates scarcity. It reassures us that we have more than we need, and there is no need to want for anything. In the continuous practice of superfluous consumption individuals and society feel 'not merely that they exist, but that they are alive'.[41]

This celebration of surplus means there is a different experience of waste in this new, affluent society. All societies, he notes, have 'wasted, squandered, expended and consumed beyond what is strictly necessary'.[42] Traditional societies attached a festive value to this kind of surplus expenditure, for example by sacrificing something valuable to highlight its symbolic importance. But modern consumer society integrates waste into the system, so it is not an effect of the system, but part of it. Products that have gone out of fashion or no longer function are destroyed in order to continue the cycle of production. Baudrillard gives the examples of breaking up old cars or recycling coffee grounds to use as fuel for trains.[43] The superfluous takes precedence over the necessary, and expenditure – buying, using, discarding consumer products – is more meaningful than the accumulation or the appropriation of these products.[44]

Unlike Marxism Baudrillard does not present consumers trapped in this system as wretched victims of big, nasty companies. Consumers willingly yield to the system in which they are integrated. We love it and want more. We submit to the gigantic code of consumption because it seems to take care of us, to give us something like a gift. We secretly hope that the consumption of signs will make us unique, different. We are grateful to advertising for taking care of us, for anticipating and addressing our needs. We cannot choose how far we wish to immerse ourselves in the system because consumption rests on a dynamic of the unlimited. Nor can we opt out of the consumer society and withdraw from this world. Consumption is, in Baudrillard's words, totalitarian, tyrannical, repressive, terrorist.

As with *The System of Objects* there is more than a trace in *The Consumer Society* of structuralism and poststructuralism, the prevailing modes of thought associated with French theory of the time. It is the system that matters, the book tells us, 'the production and the manipulation of social signifiers', rather than the consumption of any particular object itself.[45] Baudrillard's presentation of consumption as a myth we tell ourselves about ourselves recalls Barthes. Yet, unlike other thinkers of this period, he is comfortable with contradictions. He articulates oppositions rather than try to erase them. What would become a familiar Baudrillardian move, of revealing human beings trapped in a system we willingly submit to, is at the heart of *The Consumer Society*.

In 1970 Baudrillard's association with Utopie gave him another valuable opportunity: to visit the United States. He was part of a French delegation invited to that year's International Design Conference in Aspen, Colorado (IDCA). This was an august event which styled itself as marking 'a turning point in design thinking'.[46] Its theme that year was 'Environment by Design', and the French contingent – which also included the architects Jean Aubert (a fellow Utopie member) and Lionel Schein, and the designer Roger Tallon – were given a platform to debate with key figures in U.S. modern design, as well as activist architects and environmentalist collectives. Amid widespread concern about pollution in the United States at the start of the 1970s, the purpose of that year's conference was to turn the IDCA into a force that could contribute positively to improving the environment rather than continue as simply a forum for economics-based dialogue between designers, industry and government.

The French group did not share the organizers' commitment to making a more positive contribution. Instead they delivered a provocative renouncement of the very principles of the conference. Appearing on the event's final day, they issued a 'declaration' Baudrillard had been tasked with writing, entitled 'Mystique of Environment'.[47] In a comparison that would sound familiar to those versed in the celebrated Baudrillard works that would appear a decade or so later, the address referred to Aspen as 'the Disneyland of design and the environment' and contended that environmental policy was developed by governments to distract a population's attention from more important problems, such as Vietnam. Baudrillard's declaration was met with polite applause. It was not interrupted, but nor was it debated. Nevertheless, as one member of the IDCA's steering committee, the British artist Peter Blake, put it, the 'little group of French guests . . . had the last word'.[48]

For Baudrillard, the benefit of Aspen was not the opportunity it gave him to be provocative. He played down the contribution he and his compatriots made. They were 'just delegates', who 'created a "moment", a little event'. He could see that the very French 'metaphysics of revolt' were at odds with U.S. 'counter culture', and this explained the polite applause and lack of discussion after their declaration.[49] But what made the trip 'illuminating' was the opportunity it gave him to think differently about his ideas by placing them in an American context: 'America truly started things,' he said.[50] In the years to come the United States was to become increasingly important to him as both a vital, stimulating environment, and as a symbolic place: a test case for many of his arguments about society and culture.

His experience at Aspen also gave Baudrillard the kind of insight known as a negative epiphany: in teaching him what did not work, he was able to realize what did. Aspen, and indeed his work with the Utopie collective overall, merely reinforced his suspicion about the ineffectiveness of formal academic intervention on social issues. He had approved of the commitment to 'a mode of disappearance through excess' of the late 1960s and early 1970s collectives.[51] Architectural critics had argued against architecture. Urbanists were against the urban. University professors railed against the university. But by the mid-1970s there were signs that things were reverting to just what they had been before, or *reversing*. He felt that politics was dead. In any case, he felt he did not possess the required skills in pedagogy and militancy to take part fully in influential intellectual movements. He never considered himself an activist. A provocateur, yes. But Utopie, Aspen, Nanterre – all of these required an involvement in political machinations, in 'intrigue, influence, things that I was afraid of and that depressed me'.[52] He was able to stay part of Utopie for so long because it had the advantage of not really being a group. Its members did not really work together; they just met and talked, but published individually.

Barely a decade into his academic career, this was really a mourning period for Baudrillard, who felt that it was already over. Though he continued to defend sociology at Nanterre – and would do so until 1973 or 1974[53] – the atmosphere at the university after 1968 was funereal. However, he decided not to follow other major Nanterre sociologists and start afresh at Vincennes (Université Paris 8), a new university set up in 1969 in direct response to the *évènements*. By 1971 Hubert Tonka, René Lourau and Jean-François Lyotard had all made this move. Predictably, as it figured as a refuge for radical students and staff, a volatile political climate prevailed at Vincennes, but its environment also spawned some enduringly influential theoretical work. Foucault had been the first head of the philosophy department, and Hélène Cixous, Alain Badiou and Gilles Deleuze all worked there, publishing influential work during their time. Even then, Baudrillard remained ambivalent. Vincennes may have looked like a step into a new academic future, but what struck him was how it confirmed his sense that everything was in fact regressing to an old moral order. He looked on wryly – content to adopt his familiar detached-participant posture – at 'the recycling, the restoration of things, the return of the authorities to their jobs, etc.'[54] Looking back later, he felt he 'should have gone' to Vincennes but instead he 'made a bet' and stayed at Nanterre, even though life there had come to resemble 'an asylum'.[55]

Baudrillard's decision not to sever ties with Nanterre may seem like evidence of indecisiveness, a symptom of his lack of a clear disciplinary, even political, home. Conversely, it might be regarded as a decisive moment of recognition triggered by his own ferocious singularity of will. Whereas peers like Tonka chose to try – unsuccessfully in Baudrillard's view – to combine being theoretically radical and participating in a communitarian movement, this was a compromise he refused to countenance. 'I chose to distance myself. I chose to do what I wanted to do, practically alone.'[56] His wager about staying at Nanterre was that it would enable him to occupy a more comfortable metaphorical new home, which in fact had been beckoning him all along: theory. 'With theory', he reasoned, 'one can work alone, do what one wants, and, on this point, I have never compromised . . . I have never been anything but a virtual, theoretical operator, and in theory I have complete freedom.'[57]

3

Becoming 'Baudrillard': Seductions and Provocations, 1970–79

Yes, there's a kind of strategy there. I don't know how intentional. Rather, it comes as the *result* of the possibility to comprehend and take hold of the systems and to reverse them.[1]

Given Baudrillard's motivations – unconvinced by political engagement, preferring to work alone rather than as part of a collective – staying at Nanterre suited him. To belong to an institution he felt he did not really belong to helped him cultivate a sense of his own singularity in both his writing and in his vocation as an intellectual. This was to become the dominant image of Baudrillard for the rest of his career. He inhabited an 'anti-academic' persona, styling himself as 'a metaphysician, perhaps a moralist, but certainly not a sociologist'.[2] Sociology, officially his 'home' discipline as an academic, was nothing more than an arrival point, somewhere he 'landed', as if it were an airport, the gateway to exploration of the wider country.[3]

Working at Nanterre had its benefits, for his post functioned as a stable platform he could use to reach a wider audience as a public intellectual. One pleasing outcome of the transatlantic renown visited upon him by the reception of his first two books was the invitations to travel to other countries to speak. Throughout the 1970s and early 1980s Baudrillard fulfilled the duties and enjoyed the privileges of a tenured academic (albeit a rather exalted one compared to most), engaging in activities which might be considered the pinnacle of a kind of fame *within* the academy. He was invited to numerous colloquia and intellectual gatherings, spoke at international conferences and accepted invitations to appear on radio programmes such as *France Culture* or the TV discussion show *Apostrophes*.[4] This meant at times lengthy periods away from Nanterre. Students would arrive at a lecture theatre to find a note pinned up: 'Prof. Baudrillard will be back in two months.'[5]

He also continued to be remarkably prolific as a writer. In the late 1960s he had published essays in *Utopie* and other journals, as well as completing his first two books, *The System of Objects* and *The Consumer Society*, at the same time as beginning his career as a university professor. The 1970s and '80s would see no let-up in his productivity. By the time he eventually left Nanterre in 1987 Baudrillard had published ten major books as well as numerous essays. He found writing easy. He thought, he planned and then he wrote, with little editing or revision.[6]

In 1970 Baudrillard met the woman who would become his second wife. Marine Dupuis had arrived at Nanterre to study aged 25, having put off going earlier because of the post-1968 turmoil in the university system. Soon they began the relationship that was to last all of his life. Initially struck by how relaxed he was as a professor amid all the anxiety on campus, as well as by his sweet voice and the way he spoke 'without a trace of hesitation', once Marine got to know him she understood that he was 'obsessed with everything . . . obsessed with life as with a little thing that falls from the sky'.[7] She found him witty and fun-loving; the ironic tone of his writing, often overlooked by readers, was an expression of his own personality as much as a literary style. His conversation 'was light: he told you things, wonderful things, but told you so lightly, like a Zen monk'.[8] His demeanour said, 'do not take yourself seriously . . . you never felt the slightest effort in him'.[9] Marine's name was actually Martine, but Jean – perhaps playing on the fact she had returned from sailing round the world before Nanterre, and the fact that she was living on a houseboat when she started there – insisted on calling her Marine. The name stuck. Their relationship was close, and they were inseparable until the end. 'Marine is life,' he told her, which she took to mean that she figured as his 'interface' with the

Baudrillard during an appearance on the TV show *Apostrophes* in 1977.

world, a means of connecting with the vital elements of life away from thought and work.[10]

Baudrillard enjoyed being able to remain within the confines of the university but question it from within. It was a situation that neatly fitted his desire to take every opportunity 'to comprehend and take hold of the systems and to reverse them'.[11] This was to be perhaps the dominant theme of his work in the 1970s and '80s. He was fascinated with how systems are merely virtual and can therefore implode, or can actively be destabilized and made to collapse. This preoccupation cemented his sense of his destiny as a thinker, which he began to express more confidently and provocatively. As he would proclaim in one of his most famous books, *Simulacra and Simulation* (1981), 'I am a terrorist and nihilist in theory as the others are with their weapons. Theoretical violence, not truth, is the only resource left us.'[12]

Baudrillard's self-presentation as 'lone theorist' was – at least until the point when he did finally extricate himself from Nanterre – always characteristically ironic and performative. He publicly postured as a spectator of the world, observing everything, indifferent to the movements of the crowd. However, he continued to participate in collective projects, and his solitude was never as radical as he claimed. He would for instance continue working with the Utopie group until 1978, when he published his last piece in the journal. From 1975 he was closely involved with the interdisciplinary review *Traverses*, affiliated with the Centre Pompidou in Paris, and retained a position on its editorial board until 1988. *Traverses* brought together art historians, psychoanalysts, historians of religion and anthropologists to explore transformations of space in contemporary society and culture, contesting the view of space as simply a backdrop or an inert locale. Its association with this huge, self-consciously 'industrial' arts centre, known simply as Beaubourg (the area in Paris in which the Centre Pompidou was situated), was ironic given the publication in the late 1970s of Baudrillard's essay 'The Beaubourg Effect: Implosion and Deterrence', which called the edifice a 'black hole', a 'simulacrum of cultural values' because it imposed culture upon the place where culture should emerge naturally. But he thought of the journal's affiliation as 'interstitial, floating halfway in the institution'.[13]

Another reason to promote himself as a lone theorist at this time was because of the impoverished state in which he thought theory had got itself after the initial promise of 1968. Theorists in the 1970s, he felt (without specifying exactly whom he was referring to), found themselves caught between two extremes: a kind of repetitive, banal sameness, on the one side, literally 'indifferent' in his terms (which is to say, not uncaring, but saying the same thing over and over again), and an intense, passionate, yet simplistic polemicism on the other. 'In these troubled times nobody really gets to the bottom of the game any more', he felt.[14] Throughout the decade, Baudrillard himself chose to resist both extremes and to deliberately place himself on the side of 'the fatal' and the enigmatic.

The years 1973 and 1974 were when Baudrillard finally rejected radical politics and Marxism. By this point, he had decidedly 'passed to the side of theory. Leftism, or what it had become, closed militarism, was no longer an option.'[15] Some new – and what would become quintessentially 'Baudrillardian' – terms began to feature in his conference talks and radio interviews. In early October 1973, at the International Council of Societies of Industrial Design conference in Kyoto, Japan, Baudrillard spoke about 'symbolic exchange'. In 1975, in Italy, at the International Centre for Semiotics and Linguistics at the University of Urbino, he gave a seminar on 'the code and simulacra' and was invited back in successive years. He enjoyed being in Urbino and getting to know fellow attendees well – some more than others (Marine recalls seeing some pictures 'that made me think that it was a lot of fun, that he took advantage of it').[16] Baudrillard would continue speaking at Urbino at the centre's events until 1999, at the invitation of its founder, Italian poet and critic (and rector of the University of Urbino) Carlo Bo.

The System of Objects and *The Consumer Society* had been followed up by a third book, published in 1972, *For a Critique of the Political Economy of the Sign*. Made up of essays written in the late 1960s and early 1970s, when Baudrillard was completing three other books (his first two, and *The Mirror of Production* (1973)), it is a pivotal moment in the development of his body of work in the 1970s. It featured condensed versions of many of the ideas expounded in *The System of Objects* and *The Consumer Society* as well as new concepts which he would continue to explore in the work that followed, such as symbolic exchange, as well as rough outlines of themes that would be developed more fully in later work (as is clear from chapter titles such as 'The Art Auction: Sign Exchange and Sumptuary Value' or 'Requiem for the Media'). It was still received by many academics as 'squarely within Marxist thought', in that it was an attempt to further the core Marxist mission to develop a critique of political economy.[17] More precisely, it was driven by one of the key ideas of Baudrillard's early work, his conviction that the critique of political economy needed to be extended to encompass an understanding of the sign.

What he meant by this was that to fully make sense of the exchange of commodities in capitalism, we must understand it on a more virtual plane. What really operates in capitalism, in other words, is the endless exchange of signs. Marx famously thought that the 'exchange-value' of a commodity was more important than its 'use-value'. But Baudrillard contends that signs are even less 'real' and even more ambiguous than commodities or currency and therefore even more powerful: everything can be exchanged for everything else, every sign is potentially interchangeable and reversible. This exchange, these signs, are undoubtedly meaningful – but Baudrillard insists that the idea of 'meaning' is indissociable from 'value' in contemporary society. This is a far-reaching insight for Baudrillard, and one which remains vital across the span of his writings after this point, from *Symbolic Exchange and Death* (1976)

Baudrillard signing a copy of *For a Critique of the Political Economy of the Sign.*

to his later writings in the 1990s and 2000s when he would consider such events as 9/11. The problem is that modern society requires everything – every commodity, every aspect of the world – to be given an exact value, and this is the value that comes from the fact that it is a sign. In terms of political economy, it means that everything can be consumed. But more broadly it also means there is no room in the system for anything that is not accounted for in terms of an absolute designated value, such as death.

The book that appeared in 1973 is more obviously a break with Marxism than its predecessor *For a Critique of the Political Economy of the Sign*. *The Mirror of Production*, which had begun life as an essay in *Utopie* published in 1972, mounted a provocative critique of classical Marxism, accusing it of being nothing other than the mirror-image of bourgeois society because it placed production at the centre of existence and thereby normalized the capitalist system.

Symbolic Exchange and Death was more innovative and powerful, and ranks among Baudrillard's most complex and important works. It was written at a frantic pace, as if trying to meet a need for new theory to appear 'at the speed of light'.[18] It attempted a radically different way of understanding society and culture by turning both to pre-capitalist systems as models and to a range of radical and eclectic French cultural theorists and writers, such as Georges Bataille, Marcel Mauss and Alfred Jarry. *Symbolic Exchange and Death* counters the Marxist understanding of a capitalist exchange of energy, labour, utility and savings with a fundamentally human economics of excess and expenditure that renders the two – capitalist society and the human – irreconcilable. The book increased Baudrillard's reputation as a highly idiosyncratic and controversial thinker, inhabiting the margins of conventional sociology or philosophy. His work contained a dark side which did not shy away from valorizing sacrifice and death.

Symbolic Exchange and Death argues that in the modern era of the late twentieth century the last traces of the 'symbolic structure' that reigned in the pre-industrial world have all but disappeared. Marcel Mauss' famous work *The Gift* (1925) explores the way pre-capitalist society was founded upon the logic of the gift exchange rather than commodity exchange. Gift exchange is not about exchanging goods for money. It involves a three-way system of obligation: the gift must be given, received and reciprocated. Most importantly, as seen in all kinds of traditional human rituals, from harvest festivals to military service to weddings, reciprocation means effectively giving back *more* than is received, in order to avoid the receiver being fixed in an inferior position to the giver – and to ensure the triangular pattern of exchange may continue.

The idea of symbolic exchange is best conveyed by a comparison Baudrillard makes in *For a Critique of the Political Economy of the Sign* between a wedding ring and an ordinary ring. The former has symbolic value because there can be no exact equivalent in one's possessions, while the latter does not symbolize a relationship but is merely a 'personal gratification, a sign in the eyes of others'.[19] If lost, a wedding ring is irreplaceable, whereas other rings can be worn or removed or replaced because they are objects of consumption. Symbolic exchange also involves a distinctive interpersonal dimension. The symbolic act of giving causes the giver to acknowledge the fact that the consciousness of another person poses a challenge to our own consciousness. It is an act that confirms our humanness and our and the other's place in the social fabric. As in the primitive ritualistic practice of gift-giving it is not an option to avoid playing the game – for even refusing or ignoring a gift is, whether one likes it or not, a response to the challenge.

Symbolic exchange is an exchange of signs which confounds the system of complete exchangeability or reversibility of signs that defines modern capitalism. *Symbolic Exchange and Death* therefore mounts a radical challenge to Marxism, because symbolic exchange is an alternative to political economy. It is a theory which both takes account of the legacy of primitive societies and recognizes the dominant force of consumption in what Marxists would consider the phase of 'late capitalism'. What of 'death'? Death, for Baudrillard, is also an element of the symbolic. But it is treated by modern society in terms of the 'law of value'. This means it is actually ignored because the system does not ascribe any value to something which cannot be consumed, exchanged for something equivalent or accumulated. In the modern system the dead have 'no value'. Baudrillard thought that this amounted to a fundamental 'exclusion' prevailing in our society: 'the exclusion of the dead and of death'.[20] By contrast, in primitive societies, death was a challenge to life in the same manner that gift-exchange challenged people on an interpersonal level. Indeed, as Baudrillard notes, in primitive societies the dead continued to serve as 'partners' in symbolic exchange in such examples as ritual sacrifices, celebrations and feasts, occasions which would give gifts to the dead and take the 'energy' of death back into the community.

Symbolic Exchange and Death sets the scene for Baudrillard's later work. It is the bridge between his early career as an academic sociologist, and his mature phase, the point at which, as Mike Gane puts it, Baudrillard 'recast his general theory into a new vocabulary'.[21] It is the moment when Baudrillard begins to become 'Baudrillard', in other words – no longer just a leading representative of French theory but an enigmatic, provocative and, eventually, iconic figure who would become a brand of his own. The book places the emphasis, above all, on the value of objects and relationships – things that cannot be reduced to the logic of exact equivalent value which governs modern society. It also places a special importance on the poetic, which the book treats as a force with a unique subversive power (recalling its author's early formative academic interest in literary innovation) because its forms cannot be captured and valued by a system, nor reduced to equivalent exchange. Systems can be undone by the symbolic, and that includes the poetic.

The second half of the 1970s saw Baudrillard's fascination with America flourish. After Aspen in 1970 – the trip which gave him a first insight into 'another world'[22] – there were visits to New York, where he spoke at a conference at the Museum of Modern Art in 1972, and California. In 1975 he was offered a semester's teaching at the University of California, San Diego (UCSD). The invitation came from the celebrated Marxist literary theorist Fredric Jameson

– one of the first enthusiastic American readers of French theory, and instrumental in introducing the 'brand' to the United States. Jameson wanted to discuss ideas with him, or as Sylvère Lotringer would later put it, to 'pick his brains'.[23] Baudrillard was thrilled. No one knew who he was, even though his early work was beginning to be published in English (a translation of *The Mirror of Production* was released that year, 1975, by the Missouri-based Telos Press), and so there was a kind of freedom – a very American freedom – he was keen to exploit.

Baudrillard found the experience of teaching at San Diego and then Los Angeles 'eye-opening'.[24] Herbert Marcuse and Michel de Certeau were in post at UCSD when Baudrillard arrived, and Baudrillard was one of many doyens of French theory to spend

The Telos edition of *The Mirror of Production*, published in 1975.

time in California lecturing and debating. Lyotard, Derrida, Bruno Latour, Edgar Morin, and the lesser-known poststructuralist thinker Louis Marin, all came. The mid-1970s was the high point of the reception of French theory in the United States, and California, more than anywhere, the point of contact between higher education, intellectual endeavour and the countercultural spirit of the 1970s. Compared with the tumult of Nanterre, Baudrillard was struck by the 'easy-going fluid lifestyle' of the Californian campuses. His own charm and equanimity meant he fitted in well. In 1975, at UCSD's beautiful La Jolla campus by the San Diego Bay, it was an especially heady time. There were gatherings around bonfires on the beach, and trendy nightclubs. Lotringer recalled (though his account is uncorroborated) that Baudrillard 'fell passionately in love with the wife of another faculty member, and colleagues remember the pair walking barefoot in the halls of the French Department, holding hands like two flower children'.[25]

In the 1970s the United States was, like France, in the grip of its own particular generationally and politically polarized moment, post-Watergate and post-Vietnam. Political contestation was everywhere. Yet the atmosphere on campus at La Jolla somehow both reflected this and exuded a sense of being 'largely isolated from the rest of the world'.[26] Baudrillard was struck by the fact that it felt 'as though liberation were already far in the past'.[27] Even though political protest was widespread, compared to what he had experienced in Paris a few years before, the United States behaved as if it had already passed through the violent moment and was experiencing utopian liberation. This reality was actually 'hyperreal' (a produced real) in Baudrillard's developing terminology.

Baudrillard loved the United States, especially the empty, apparently transient communities he visited while working in San Diego. Lotringer commented that he 'was as much a Californian as a Frenchman could ever be: low-key, relaxed, and soft-spoken'.[28] Yet he never seriously considered emigrating to the United States, even when he was eventually free of his commitments to Nanterre in the late 1980s. Remaining a French resident was 'an automatic choice, out of inertia', he later said. 'So what – I'm European.'[29] But he was always at pains to point out – especially after the publication of his ground-breaking book, *America*, in 1986 – that he never had any desire to compare the United States with Europe, along the lines of the established European literary tradition of writers visiting the United States and 'reporting back' to their countrymen (Alexis de Tocqueville, D. H. Lawrence, G. K. Chesterton, Jean-Paul Sartre and others). Nor did he wish to grasp the 'essence' of America. He later reflected:

> What I was observing was another scene, a primal scene . . . For me it was a kind of otherness or fascination. It wasn't the political or economic reality which interested me, but that sort of transfiguration of banality characteristic of a new continent – not just new geographically, but mentally. I experienced it on a cinema screen, as it were, hypothesizing almost experimentally a country without a history.[30]

As 'primal scene', the United States was often a touchstone for Baudrillard's interpretation of contemporary reality, providing ready examples of what he was diagnosing. Thinking back to his experiences in the French academic landscape in the late 1960s and '70s, for example, he said, 'One didn't have to wait for the year 2000 to perceive all that was going to take place,' referring to one of the 'extreme phenomena' (the millennium) he would write about.[31] You only had to look at what was really happening in the United States.

The relationship between Baudrillard and Jameson had apparently soured by 1976. According to Lotringer, Jameson was by then advising his students not to attend lectures given by anyone in 'the French camp'.[32] But Baudrillard's residencies at the University of California (a second would come in 1977, this time at UCLA, and he would continue to teach off and on at Santa Barbara until 1986) also occasioned other significant personal encounters, mainly with other French intellectuals rather than American academics (whom he would later dismiss as 'these Californian scholars with monomaniacal passions for things French or Marxist').[33] It was in LA, in the summer of 1977, that he had first

Californian desert, by Baudrillard. The 1970s was the beginning of Baudrillard's fascination with America.

met Lotringer, a compatriot exile who was to become a lifelong friend, ally and collaborator, instrumental in championing and interpreting Baudrillard's work in the United States. They went for a long walk on the beach at Marina del Rey in Venice close to LAX, 'past manicured lawns and tanned joggers exhibiting their vacuous physicality'.[34] It was in California that Baudrillard, along with Certeau and Marin, the art critics Gilbert Lascault and Marc Le Bot, and the philosopher Paul Virilio (who was also to become a lifelong friend), founded *Traverses*. In California Baudrillard also met the English novelist J. G. Ballard, whose surreal 1970s fictions such as *Crash* (1973) and *Concrete Island* (1974) were in tune with Baudrillard's perspective on the world and many of his ideas. He wrote about *Crash* (calling it 'the first great novel of the universe of simulation') in an essay that was first published in 1976 and subsequently appeared in *Simulacra and Simulation* in 1981.[35] The two men corresponded briefly after this, though it was not a friendship that endured especially long.

Both *The Mirror of Production* and *Symbolic Exchange and Death* call for a new mode of theorizing that 'will bring all the force and questioning of primitive societies to bear on Marxism and psychoanalysis', turning the tables on the familiar Western conceit that assumes its dominant theoretical discourses can confidently diagnose the primitive.[36] Yet while both texts voice explicitly Baudrillard's desire to 'break this fascination, this self-fetishization of Western thought', he felt that neither book – even the more ambitious *Symbolic Exchange and Death* – actually *performed* this challenge, in the way they were written.[37] Although it had been completed 'feverishly' before he left San Diego in 1975, *Symbolic Exchange and Death* was not itself a theoretical equivalent of a more 'primitive' kind of writing.[38] It is poetic neither in form nor style.

The desire to perform a critique rather than simply expound one had much to do with Baudrillard's next book, *Forget Foucault* (1977). This provocative title still amounts to one of his most audacious moves – the first time he had chosen to mount this kind of challenge. He would do something similar in later work such as 'The Gulf War Will Not Take Place' (1991) and 'The Spirit of Terrorism' (2002).[39] But the fact that *Forget Foucault* directs its provocation towards one thinker in particular, especially at the highpoint of his influence and that of French theory itself, proved especially controversial.

Forget Foucault began life as an article commissioned by Jean Piel, the editor of the journal *Critique*, who asked Baudrillard if he wanted to respond to the publication of Foucault's 1976 book *The Will to Knowledge*, the first of the four volumes of his acclaimed *History of Sexuality*. Baudrillard wrote a piece, and Piel duly sent it to a number of reviewers – including Foucault himself. At first Foucault reacted well. He read the essay and met with Baudrillard for three hours, discussing the issues it raised. Foucault told Baudrillard he wanted to write a response. In anticipation Baudrillard then withdrew his article from circulation so he could amend it if necessary and the two pieces could be published together. After a month, however, things had changed. Foucault informed Baudrillard he no longer wished to respond and told him he could go ahead and do whatever he wanted with the essay.

It was never published in *Critique*. Instead Éditions Galilée published it on 24 March 1977 as a slim stand-alone volume. When the book appeared Baudrillard recalled that Foucault 'suddenly became furious'.[40] It turned out he had not taken kindly to Baudrillard's polemic. He dismissed the publication by saying, 'I would have more problems remembering Baudrillard.'[41] Privately Foucault was more hurt by the criticisms than he let on.[42] The rumour was that when the book appeared, he immediately sent his students to the bookshops in the 5th and 6th arrondissements of Paris to buy all available copies so no one could get their hands on it.

Whatever its object really felt, the book reinforced the impression of Baudrillard as outsider-within, and had profound and lasting implications for his career. Parisian intellectuals regarded him as a traitor. Gilles Deleuze – who is also a partial object of Baudrillard's critique in the book – and his co-writer Félix Guattari (Baudrillard's fellow Maoist a decade previously, now estranged) considered it a shameful and irresponsible act, even though they had their own philosophical disagreements with Foucault. It was the style of the provocation that mattered, more than the content. Baudrillard's excommunication from French intellectual circles was all the more symbolic as he was in Los Angeles at the time of its publication. As Lotringer wryly noted, 'French ostracism still had an effect some six thousand miles away, like the moon on the distant Pacific shores.'[43] For years Lotringer did not dare mention to Deleuze his new friendship with Baudrillard – despite his certainty that Baudrillard was precisely the kind of counter-capitalist hero held up as a model in Deleuze and Guattari's famous 1972 book *Anti-Oedipus*. Ten years after *Forget Foucault*, in the late 1980s, Baudrillard confessed he still felt 'quarantined' as a result of the influence of Foucault allies in the university system and the media.[44]

It is not surprising that a self-conscious outsider of the Paris intellectual scene would harbour a desire to knock someone like Michel Foucault from his pedestal. While controversial and undoubtedly more than a little outside the norm himself, Foucault's academic career was nevertheless the epitome of academic establishment success. In 1970 he had been appointed to perhaps the most prestigious academic position in France, Professor at the Collège de France, for a newly named Chair in the History of Systems of Thought – and at the age of just 44. Despite being only three years younger, Baudrillard had of course taken much longer to get into university teaching, and via an unorthodox route. It is equally unsurprising that Foucault would refuse to elevate the profile of an upstart theorist – one arrogant enough to believe he could persuade people to 'forget Foucault' in a mere fifty-page essay[45] – by writing a response to it.

Yet while there was surely a tinge of *ressentiment* to its publication, *Forget Foucault* was not primarily an expression of personal grievance on Baudrillard's part. As he later observed, the book's title was in fact far more provocative than the text itself; the actual critique did not contain any personal attacks.[46] The book is best made sense of as an example of Baudrillard's commitment to his mission to work alone, 'on the side of theory', rather than to observe the niceties of conventional academic argument-building and debate. *Forget Foucault* was a challenge of the kind Baudrillard had written about in *Symbolic Exchange and Death*, one laid down to its eponymous philosopher but also to the intellectual establishment as a whole. Foucault's decision not to write a response trapped him in the logic of symbolic exchange: not responding was itself a clear rebuttal.

The book showed that Baudrillard had found a way to harness the pataphysical spirit that had spurred him on intellectually from the outset and to use it in his theoretical writing. The text challenged the philosopher who was at the time perhaps the most influential of all, even 'untouchable'.[47] It took on Foucault's key ideas surrounding power and sex, and pushed them so far that they reversed themselves:

> I've always greatly admired Foucault. But that was just the point. The perfection of his analysis of power had something troubling about it, or at least something that deserved to be explored as the reverse side of a perfect picture. That's what I tried to do,

sincerely believing (though, I admit, naïvely) that this type of confrontation was worth having.[48]

It would be unrealistic to enter into the pataphysical mode without accepting that any critique you mount is likely to be hampered by its own potential to implode. Baudrillard acknowledged his challenge to Foucault might itself be regarded as pompous. So he liked Lotringer's idea of adding a supplement to *Forget Foucault* when it was eventually published in an English-language version (in 1987 as part of Lotringer's 'Foreign Agents' Semiotext(e) series): a lengthy interview entitled 'Forget Baudrillard'. The point about reversibility was emphasized by giving the volume a double cover which read *Forget Foucault* on one side and *Forget Baudrillard* on the other. Baudrillard was always comfortable indulging in self-puncturing irony. He later joked he had planned a whole series of 'Forget' books, covering other thinkers such as Lacan, and when it was complete he would have begun the 'Remember' series: '*Remember Baudrillard*, etc. It would have been a huge success and it would have lasted a very long time.'[49]

Forget Foucault tends to be overlooked when it comes to Baudrillard's most important books, even though Lotringer maintained it was 'by far the best introduction to Baudrillard's work'.[50] One of its objectives was to remove the influence of Foucault from Baudrillard's own work, just as he had done with conventional sociology and Marxism. *Symbolic Exchange and Death*'s account of how death in modernity was cast outside the system, no longer considered a 'normal' part of existence, drew on Foucault's *Madness and Civilization* (1961). The book also sketches out a history of simulation that resembles Foucault's 'genealogical' approach to history (influenced in turn by Nietzsche), looking to breaks or anomalies to explain historical change rather than concentrating on continuity. But *Forget Foucault* is the foundation for some of the distinctively Baudrillardian ideas which feature in books that came after. As well as simulation, the book considered the interplay between 'production' and 'seduction'. The term 'production' has an expanded sense in Baudrillard's thinking. It both includes the purely industrial sense of the term, that is, the production of objects, or mass production, and expands beyond it to refer to the production of reality, which in the modern era is simulated. Reality is not simply 'there', for human beings to 'enter' or live inside. Rather it is something produced by the order of value he had written about in *Symbolic Exchange and Death*.

The opposite force to production is seduction. Where production brings things forward, manufactures them, gives them a value, seduction is a process 'of diverting them from that value, and hence from their identity, their reality, to destine them for the play of appearances, for their symbolic exchange'.[51] Seduction enables the logic of production to be challenged, continually shadowing or haunting it. It works according to invisibility and ambivalence, and thus threatens to cause systems to implode and go into reverse. An example of this process is psychoanalysis, which operates according to the principles of production in that it is designed to bring into the light the hidden motivating factors behind individual behaviour. It therefore *produces* a reality which can be interpreted or treated. Yet the very object of study of psychoanalysis, the unconscious, which Freud proudly 'discovered' in the late nineteenth century, is essentially a *seductive* organism which generates signs that divert analysis, leading subjects on, leading them astray. Baudrillard argues that Freud noticed this himself at the very beginning, only to take a wrong turn. Psychoanalysis began with his 'seduction theory', but Freud famously abandoned this in 1907 and developed instead 'a machinery of interpretation . . . that offer[s] all the characteristics of objectivity and coherence'. As a result, Freud actually ensured seduction would forever haunt psychoanalysis, continually re-emerging 'within the course of every cure'.[52]

This critique of Freud features in Baudrillard's book *Seduction*, initially published by Éditions Galilée in 1979. It continues his method of exposing the logic of a particular system of thought and showing how its proponents did all they could to prevent their system from turning back on itself. It makes a similar case about the linguistic theory of Ferdinand de Saussure (a huge influence on structuralism) and repeats Baudrillard's critique of Foucault. But there is something different about *Seduction*, something unlike even *Symbolic Exchange and Death* and *Forget Foucault*; it is more personal and even less observant of the academic conventions of writing. It reads as if Baudrillard is trying to grasp something for his own satisfaction. The book's original French title was *De la séduction* (On Seduction). The preposition makes little difference ultimately, but it does imply that Baudrillard is writing about a force which eludes him, something he cannot fully possess.

This kind of writing is the gateway to Baudrillard's mature, recognizably 'Baudrillardian' phrase. Before *Seduction* he thought he had written in a 'rather offhand manner'. But from this book onward his writing became infused with a 'vital necessity' because he found a way of involving his 'own life' in what he wrote.[53] By this he did not mean writing anything that resembled autobiography, nor providing his texts with 'why I write' supplements. It was about finally casting off the established mode of academic writing, 'that sort of distancing, critical and analytical at the same time, that allows you to "explain" things'. His alternative was to treat as 'exterior' both world and himself as writer: 'whilst out there [in writing], everything is all right: you are not divided. What you write describes what you are.'[54]

Seduction animates Baudrillard's fascination with how the object, so often secondary to the subject in philosophy and other disciplines, is something that has a kind of agency of its own. It can lay false trails, lead the subject on, point to but preserve the secret. It belongs to a different 'order', the realm of enchantment, of secrets, of the poetic – anything which opposes the 'banal'. More than anything seduction is ironic. It exposes, undoes, reverses, makes fun. Seduction is a broad-ranging principle in Baudrillard. He thought of it as a 'form', or something that shaped or was visible in particular relationships (between people, between a work of art and its viewer or reader, and so forth). It was a challenge, a pact, or an alliance, manifested typically in the guise of 'an enigmatic duel', 'a violent solicitation or attraction'.[55] Seduction is a historical form that emerged in what Baudrillard considered a 'golden age' of seduction, the Renaissance to the eighteenth century, and is best considered 'a game of strategy without any special connection to love'.[56]

Yet, problematically, he presents it at certain points as 'a feminine principle'. This was not received well by many female readers and writers. The prominent feminist philosopher Luce Irigaray took immediate exception to the book's use of a misogynist work like Søren Kierkegaard's *Diary of a Seducer* (1843) to exemplify his concept of seduction.[57] Seduction may well be a more general form, but specific examples involving women who either seduce or are seduced – such as *Diary of a Seducer* – also evoke tired and dangerous stereotypes of woman as man's 'other'. Similarly, positioning 'the feminine' on the side of the 'object' makes sense in terms of Baudrillard's theory, but veers too closely towards the misogynist habit of objectifying women.

Any retrospective analysis of Baudrillard from the point of view of gender needs to reckon with rhetorical gambits which are undoubtedly misogynistic. At one point in his 1983 book *Fatal Strategies* he muses, 'Women are so skilled, they seem to be so submissive, they know so well, too well, how to be unhappy – there must be something there that is hiding and lying in wait.'[58] An even more notorious and indefensible comment (again despite the broader significance of sacrifice in his system or the sense that the 'object' of the desert is what makes the demand) is made in *America*, when he writes, about Death Valley, that, 'You always have to bring something into the desert to sacrifice, and offer it to the desert as a victim. A woman. If something has to disappear, something matching the desert for beauty, why not a woman?'[59] In spite of the enduring value of Baudrillard's theories and his writings, and his preference for provocation over invocation, on some issues he will continue to be associated with retrograde attitudes.

Baudrillard regretted what he characterized as 'dreadful misunderstandings' in such feminist objections to his concept of seduction. He tried to clarify that his argument was not intended to 'push women back' into purely a 'seductive' role, but actually had a pro-feminist impulse. It was an acknowledgement that women historically have *responded* to being pushed back by patriarchy through irony or derision (that is, seductive mechanisms), and that this resistance had fuelled feminist critique of the kind that Irigaray's work itself exemplified. 'Seduction is a subversive power, it makes it possible to have mastery over that rather secret rule of the game, mastery not of power relations but another type of relationship,' he said.[60] A person of any gender can be part of a seductive challenge; the seduction is not issuing from that person due to their identity. Such protestations have been used in efforts to rehabilitate Baudrillard's perspective on women and femininity.[61] But the fact is that, for all his denials and his attempt to hide behind a form of conceptual irony, there is something deeply ambiguous and anti-feminist in his remarks, which need to be kept in mind while understanding how important a form seduction remained to Baudrillard. The concept cannot be cleansed of his misogynistic formulations, even though seduction – and related ideas about games, secrets and destiny – always remained positive values in his writing because they promise an alternative to the rigid, reversible systems he critiques, an alternative to the banality of the world as he saw it, as well as much criticism and philosophy.

4

Life on the Other Side: Art and America, 1980–86

> I observe, I accept, I assume the immense process of the destruction of appearances (and of the seduction of appearances) in the service of meaning (representation, history, criticism, etc.) . . . I observe, I accept, I assume, I analyze the second revolution, that of the twentieth century, that of postmodernity, which is the immense process of the destruction of meaning, equal to the earlier destruction of appearances.[1]

Back in France, during the late 1970s and early 1980s, Baudrillard must have been struck by the contrast between his excommunication from French academia following the furore surrounding *Forget Foucault*, and the growing appreciation of his work in America. His stints at the University of California, and the English translations of *The Consumer Society* and *The Mirror of Production*, which were being widely read alongside Barthes' *Mythologies* and Foucault's *Discipline and Punish*, meant his international renown was growing. Professionally, he existed in Paris as a kind of internal exile, still teaching at Nanterre, writing fluidly and prolifically, but increasingly pitching his work towards a readership outside France.

By the early 1980s Baudrillard was regarded as one of the most prominent representatives of the group of French theorists influencing the United States. The Europe-leaning political and social theory journal *Telos* had been, from the mid-1970s, a platform for North American thinkers to engage with his work, and in 1981 its publishing wing, Telos Press Publishing, followed up its 1975 translation of *The Mirror of Production* with a translation of *For a*

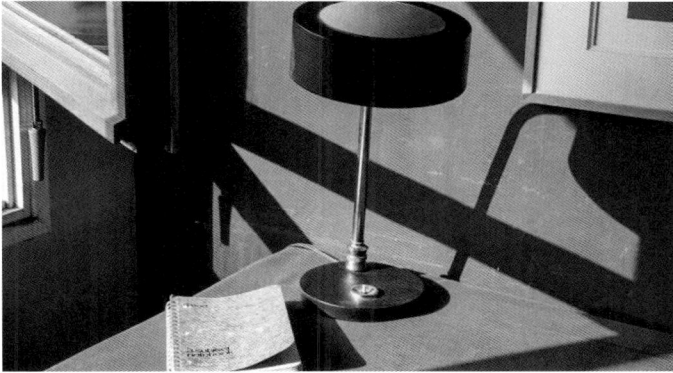

Baudrillard, *Paris, 1986*, photograph.

Political Economy of the Sign. Baudrillard's notion of simulation, advanced in both of these books (and a term first mentioned in *The Consumer Society* back in 1970), was particularly appealing to American cultural and sociological theorists who felt that the current nature of mass culture and politics was nullifying any form of meaningful critique. While no more optimistic in their conclusions, Baudrillard's early theories of the sign offered a powerful explanation of the homogenizing effect of media communications.

Baudrillard's next work, 1981's *Simulacra and Simulation*, expands further on his notion of simulation. It remains one of his most cited books. It is also, more than any other, the Baudrillard text that has been linked to postmodernism – a context which always puzzled Baudrillard because postmodernism was such an indistinct term, even though he would occasionally use it himself. In *Simulacra and Simulation* he makes a pledge to 'observe, accept, assume, analyse' 'the second revolution . . . that of postmodernity', which reads like a call to arms, perhaps even a catechism. It is the book that would both inspire and appear in the 1999 sci-fi film *The Matrix*.

Simulacra and Simulation is user-friendly. It comprises mainly short chapters with pithy titles which deliver authoritative and original analyses of examples of 1970s culture. Like most of

Baudrillard's books it is a collection or recollection of material (essays, articles, notes, lectures) he had produced before. This pattern of self-recycling can make Baudrillard's project overall – as detractors have often argued – seem like one vast, never-ending conversation or monologue. But it accurately reflects the consistency of his preoccupations, as well as his conviction that 'one has but one idea in one's life.' The difference from his previous works was that *Simulacra and Simulation* looked like a collection of linked essays, and this made it more accessible and different to anything Baudrillard had yet published. It was both more structured and looser than *Seduction*. It invited readers to dip in and out, to start with any chapter they liked. Its chapters covered such cultural production as the films *Apocalypse Now* (1979, dir. Francis Ford Coppola), J. G. Ballard's novel *Crash*, the 1973 TV documentary series *An American Family* (in many ways the precursor of reality TV in the twenty-first century) and a diverse range of cultural phenomena ranging from Disneyland to advertising to the science of cloning.

The book is preoccupied with the hyperreal effects of modern electronic media, and especially the idea of how reality is produced by the real. Between its covers are some of the lines that would end up being Baudrillard's most quoted over the next decades, despite all of the many books that would follow:

the desert of the real[2]

Disneyland exists in order to hide that it is the 'real' country, all of 'real' America that is Disneyland.[3]

We live in a world where there is more and more information, and less and less meaning.[4]

The impression is that this is Baudrillard writing from a detached, futuristic vantage-point where he can survey or travel through popular culture at will, exposing, as Barthes did in *Mythologies*, profound truths about our society we would all know are true if we only knew how and where to look.

A full-length English translation of *Simulacra and Simulation* would not become available until 1994, though many of its sections appeared independently before then. What made it such a success was the publication of *Simulations* in 1983 by Sylvère Lotringer's Semiotext(e) imprint. *Simulations* was a book tailored specifically for the North American market. It was a curiosity; a translation of a text that had never before existed in that form. Lotringer had set the lengthiest and most important essay in *Simulacra and Simulation*, 'The Precession of Simulacra', alongside 'The Orders of Simulacra' from *Symbolic Exchange and Death*, to create a mini 'greatest hits' volume which gave the impression of drawing together the strands of Baudrillard's work so far, both for a readership that knew of him and for one ready to discover him. Until this point readers of Baudrillard were mainly students and academics citing his work as part of sociological and political theory. But *Simulations* was to give him a far broader, eventually global, reach.

'The Precession of Simulacra', the first of its two sections, is one of the foundational essays for anyone seeking to understand Baudrillard's thought. Its subject is summed up by another line that would become one of his most quoted, a metaphor about the way reality is produced by representation: it is 'the map that precedes the territory'.[5] Where once the territory came before the map, or at least 'survived it' (or remained present even though the map was what mattered), Baudrillard contended that in our era the territory is actually produced by the map. In making the analogy, he was alluding to the Argentinian writer Jorge Luis Borges's 1946 one-paragraph short story 'On Exactitude in Science'.[6] This text is presented in Borges's characteristic pseudo-academic style as a snippet from an obscure 1658 travelogue, telling of an unidentified Western civilization that had once developed cartography to the stage where maps were so huge and perfect they covered the exact space of cities and provinces: the entire empire itself. But later generations lost interest and abandoned the project, leaving these vast maps to become rotted by the elements until all that remained were 'tattered ruins' which were still 'inhabited by animals and beggars'.[7] The implication is that because these maps covered the

Jean Baudrillard, 1 February 1983.

terrain they represented so absolutely they had once reached a point where they themselves were populated by every living creature.

This is the perfect metaphor for Baudrillard's understanding of the process of simulation, only in reverse. In the contemporary world, he argued, now

> it is the map that precedes the territory – precession of simulacra – it is the map that engenders the territory and if we were to revive [Borges's] fable, it would be the territory whose shreds are slowly rotting across the map. It is the real, and not the map, whose vestiges subsist here and there, in the deserts which are no longer those of the Empire, but our own.[8]

Simulation is a rendering of the real that covers the real almost completely; the 'tattered ruins' of the real can be glimpsed only at certain points through the 'map', in elements Baudrillard calls, in the original version of the essay (the phrase that would be used in *The Matrix*), 'the desert of the real'. 'Simulation is no longer that of a territory, a referential being or a substance [but] the generation by models of a real without origin or reality: a hyperreal.'[9]

'The Precession of Simulacra' is a complex, foundational text in Baudrillard's theory, which is also – as befits the new prose style he deployed from *Seduction* onwards – elliptical and ironic. Humour is never far from the surface, as the epigraph to the essay, which Baudrillard references as being a quotation from Ecclesiastes in the Old Testament, shows:

> The simulacrum is never what hides the truth – it is truth that hides the fact that there is none.
> The simulacrum is true.

But these lines are not to be found in the Bible. Baudrillard made them up – indulging in a little simulation of his own.

The reframing of a freshly translated 'The Orders of Simulacra' as the second part of *Simulations* complemented 'The Precession of Simulacra' by providing Baudrillard's Foucauldian historical model of the simulacrum as a supplementary analysis of 'the three orders of appearance', or ways in which imitations of reality have prepared for the current dominance of simulation:

> 1. the natural law of 'the counterfeit', 'the dominant scheme of the "classical" period, from the Renaissance to the industrial revolution'; which is superseded by
> 2. the commercial or market law of 'production', 'the dominant scheme of the industrial era'; which in turns gives way to
> 3. the structural law of 'simulation', 'the reigning scheme of the current phase that is controlled by the code'.[10]

Simulation is undoubtedly the most commonly misunderstood aspect of Baudrillard's thought, even among those who respond to it enthusiastically. The assumption is often that he is arguing that copies of things in the world have come to take the place of the real things they imitate. The hypothesis that there are two levels of existence (a level in which we live, in reality, and a level in which we exist virtually) is more in tune with an essentially Platonic boundary between the real or ideal world and the world of images or forms, or even Jacques Lacan's psychoanalytic orders of imaginary, symbolic and real. The implication is that the real world still exists, unaltered, behind the hyperreal cover or map. But Baudrillard's argument is more radical. The real itself is simulated. This means that we produce the real as pre-coded signs which function *as* the real. It is not about the double or the copy standing in for or being indistinguishable from the original (a tenet of postmodernism), but about the way the real itself is generated by models with neither origin nor reality.

Simulations was published in 1983 as part of the first three books in what was to become a hugely successful, influential and long-running series from Semiotext(e), 'Foreign Agents'. The others were Deleuze and Guattari's *On the Line* and Paul Virilio's *Pure War* (both also published in 1983). Given the influence Baudrillard's volume was to have, the idea of pairing 'The Precession of Simulacra' and 'The Orders of Simulacra' seems especially inspired, but it was also somewhat fortuitous. Lotringer had originally planned to go with *Forget Foucault*, but realized he had better put this on hold because Deleuze and Guattari, still smarting from the actions of the man who had become 'the shame of the profession' in 1977, told him they would refuse to publish with Semiotext(e) if he did.[11]

The idea for the 'Foreign Agents' series had come about when Lotringer sensed the influence of the original *Semiotext(e)* art journal, which he had co-founded in 1973, was on the wane. He decided to move on to publishing works in translation, mainly by French thinkers. The volumes were eye-catching little black books, which deliberately contained no introductions, no afterwords and no clarifications. Lotringer thought of them as 'theory-brut', drawing on the connotation of champagne as both high-quality and dry, raw and direct. They were meant to be read by dipping in and out while on the move, on the subway or in cafés, to be placed 'in the pockets of spiked leather jackets as much as on the shelves'.[12]

Lotringer did much to promote the work of a number of French intellectuals in the English-speaking world in the 1980s through his 'Foreign Agents' series: Deleuze and Guattari, Lyotard,

Foucault, Virilio. But Baudrillard was always the thinker most famously associated with Semiotext(e). After *Simulations*, many of his important 1980s works appeared under the 'Foreign Agents' banner. In 1983 Lotringer published a translation of Baudrillard's 1978 book *In the Shadow of the Silent Majorities*, an important precursor to some of his later works which focused on the role of the 'mass majority' in politics, the fact that the concept had no critical value but was a space where critique was in fact swallowed up and dulled. It was a deliberate 'calling to account' of sociology.[13] The book also explored the role of terrorism in society. Other short books followed: *Forget Foucault* (complete with reversible double-cover) finally appeared in 1987, and *The Ecstasy of Communication* (originally *L'Autre par lui-même*) was published in 1988.

Baudrillard and Lotringer were clearly kindred spirits. Lotringer was younger by nearly ten years and had a similar 'insider-outsider' intellectual background, having studied with Barthes at the École pratique des hautes études in the mid-1960s, then working at the Sorbonne before moving to Columbia University, New York, in the early 1970s. Their friendship had strengthened since that first walk on the beach at UCLA in 1977. Lotringer showed Jean and Marine around New York, taking them to vibrant nightclubs and avant-garde venues. He appreciated that the key to understanding Baudrillard's thought was his pataphysical grounding. Because of his interest in the U.S. art scene (art students were seemingly always more receptive to theoretical ideas and willing to incorporate them in their practice), Lotringer also recognized that the trick to promoting theory was not simply making new contributions to knowledge available to researchers. The philosopher Richard Hertz said that what distinguished Baudrillard and Lotringer from many of their theory peers was their understanding that 'theory is all very nice but it's not an end in itself, it has to integrate into one's life. It has to make a difference somewhere; it's not about endless word mongering.'[14]

Nevertheless the success of *Simulations* was not immediate. Six months after it had appeared (in January 1983), Lotringer arranged for Baudrillard to do a lecture tour in the United States to promote his ideas, booking events at a number of Ivy League universities. But the tour was disastrous. Barely anyone turned up. This prompted Lotringer, ever the intellectual entrepreneur, to go back to a community he knew well, the American art world, to promote Baudrillard's work, targeting artists and curators in particular. His instinct was sound. Many young American artists felt they needed a new way to articulate their dismay at capitalism, especially faced with the accumulative, aggressive corporate strategies of the Reagan administration. Because capitalism absorbed everything, Lotringer wrote, the theoretical challenge was how 'to counter it *from within*, redirecting its flows, ceaselessly moving ground'.[15] *Simulations*

Sylvère Lotringer, 1992.

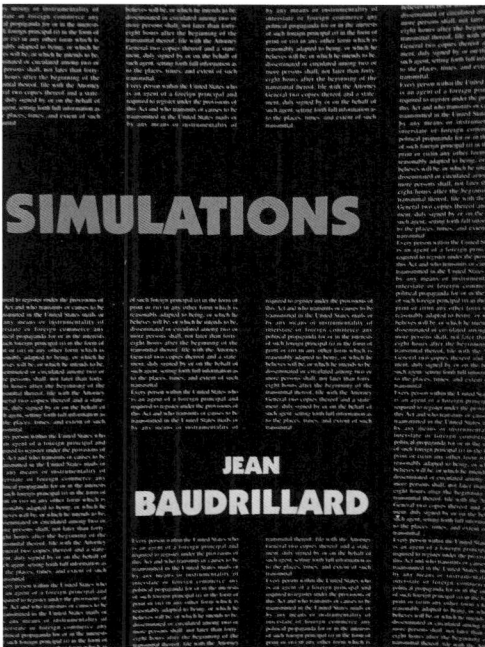

The 1983 Semiotext(e) edition of *Simulations*: within two years of its publication, 'everyone had read *Simulations*.'

SIMULATIONS

JEAN BAUDRILLARD

was one of the texts that seemed, excitingly, to promise a way to do this, as well as salving the postmodern sensation of exhaustion that nagged at many contemporary artists: the recognition that it was impossible to produce original artwork in a late capitalist world where everything was endlessly and perfectly reproducible. One curator told Lotringer that within two years of its publication 'everyone had read *Simulations*.'[16]

Lotringer's pairing of the essays in *Simulations* made the book seem like a work of 'pop philosophy', deceptively accessible and simplistic on the surface (though it was in fact complex and required the context of Baudrillard's wider theoretical system to be fully understood). Chris Kraus (who married Lotringer in 1988) thought the key to the book's success at that precise cultural moment was because it 'read less as a philosophical treatise than as a manifesto'.[17] Her insight applies more broadly, to the declarative, enigmatic quality of Baudrillard's style deployed in most of his work from *Seduction* onwards. But, packaged in its concise, cool Semiotext(e) format, Baudrillard's prose in *Simulations* read like a declaration of intent, an exhortation to readers to follow him:

> Each phrase, at that time, felt completely portentous, and artists memorized shards of the book as ominous koans: 'To seek blood in its own death, to renew the cycle by the mirror of crisis, negativity, and anti-power: this is the only alibi of every power, of every institution attempting to break the vicious circle of its irresponsibility and its fundamental non-existence, of its déjà-vu and its déjà-mort.'[18]

Baudrillard's notion of simulation was considered a frame for understanding the work of American 'identity artists' such as Sherrie Levine and Cindy Sherman, who provocatively explored individual style and original authorship, and also the work of the socio-feminist conceptual collage-artist Barbara Kruger (who had acknowledged the influence of *The Mirror of Production* on her art).[19] But it was more directly influential among the so-called 'Neo-Geo' ('Geo' being 'geometrists') collective of New York artists – known by some as the 'Simulationists' – such as Peter Halley, Ashley Bickerton and Jeff Koons, who appropriated the aesthetics of media and commodification to engineer a kind of reversibility. In a 1984 essay Halley cited Baudrillard's concepts approvingly.[20] The *New Yorker*'s art critic, Peter Schjeldahl, described the autumn of 1986 as the 'season of simulationism'.[21]

Baudrillard himself, predictably, was nonplussed by this association. He was sceptical about the possibility of effective critique from within, for he was convinced this always became absorbed by what it was trying to critique. He also felt the 'Simulationists' had misunderstood his idea of simulation, treating it in essentially Platonic terms as simply an illusion to be compared with what is real. His alternative to a critique from within was to push the logic of a system as far as it could go, to force it to reckon with its contradictions, or to implode.

This was the impulse behind the explorations in his book *Fatal Strategies*, published in France in the same year as *Simulations*, though not in translation until 1990. While Baudrillard had always been fascinated by the object, and since the late 1970s had sought deliberately to position himself on the side of the object rather than to analyse any object or 'system' of objects from a detached perspective, *Fatal Strategies* was his most radical attempt yet to do this. The book stages a series of encounters with the object which shows how it traps the subject in a 'fatal strategy'. These include analyses of Tiresias, pornography, hostages, animals, Alphonse Allais' story 'Only in Paris', and Kierkegaard's *Diary of a Seducer* (again). The object is imagined as having its own ironic agency, even passion. It is not passive, but nor is it an anthropomorphized 'subject'.

The term 'fatal' is related to destiny and also death, often in the form of implosion. Baudrillard set what he dismissed as 'banal theory' against the 'fatal theory' to which he had committed in the 1980s: 'in the first the subject believes himself [*sic*] to be cleverer than the object; in the second the object is always supposed to be cleverer, more cynical and more inspired than the subject, whom he awaits ironically at the end of the detour.'[22] *Fatal Strategies* needs to be understood in this context. It also means recognizing that theory itself – Baudrillard's theory, too – has a particular relation to the object. This is why *Fatal Strategies* is also a particularly personal book in the non-autobiographical manner of incorporating Baudrillard's 'own life' into his theory which characterizes *Seduction*. He did not disagree when one interviewer described *Fatal Strategies* as 'a treatise on your own personal metamorphosis, a sort of "Confessions of a fin-de-siècle intellectual"'.[23]

Fatal Strategies includes an essay in which Baudrillard engages with the work of the French conceptual artist Sophie Calle. Calle was, at the time, categorized alongside other 1980s artists whose work either exemplified or was influenced by simulation, such as Levine or Sherman. Yet she was one of the few contemporary artists Baudrillard admired without qualification because her work allowed itself to surrender completely to seduction. A version of his piece about her appeared separately in a joint 1983 publication, *Suite vénetienne / Please Follow Me*. It is prudent, given Calle's fondness for autofiction, to take with a pinch of salt her claim that during her time as a sociology student at Nanterre in the 1960s Baudrillard agreed to let her pass her exams to pacify her father so he would 'let her escape around the world'.[24] Nevertheless they would stay friends for decades, and Baudrillard would jokingly send her the Chinese translation of each of his books when it was published – acknowledging he knew well she would not read nor understand his work anyway.

'Venetian Suite' was the photographic and textual documentation of a project Calle had embarked upon in 1979, when she followed a man to Venice, known only as Henri B., having only met him once at a party where he happened to mention his forthcoming trip. She tracked him down and followed him for thirteen days, compiling an extensive dossier about his movements and her pursuit, accompanied by photographs. Throughout it all, Calle repeatedly denied possible motivations for her behaviour. She was not interested in Henri B., nor his feelings. She was not in love with him, even though at times it felt like pursuing a lover. She did not intend to uncover his 'secret life'. The story resembles a deconstructed noir detective story, or a love story. But Calle resisted imposing a narrative on her activities by wondering what the outcome might be, and was adamant that she did not even intend to produce a work of art, for it all happened before she considered herself an artist.[25] She was as much at the mercy of the project's mystery as Henri B.

Calle's pursuit, Baudrillard thought, relieved her quarry of 'the responsibility for his own life', for it is as if she is responsible for him, like an anxious mother shadowing her child who has wandered away from home, thinking he is alone.[26] And, paradoxically, this means that she is simultaneously relieved of the responsibility for her own life, too, for all her energies are channelled simply into the act of following the unpredictable movements of another. The beauty of this game, for Baudrillard, is that it causes one of the prevailing myths of Western culture to implode: that we are unique, separate, autonomous beings, in charge of our own destiny. Our pretensions to uniqueness are made to seem ridiculous when we are doubled in this way, as when someone makes fun of another by mimicking them. But, more seriously, our will and our desires are what make us individuals. When these are negated, so is our sense of individuality.

The reception of *Simulations* by artists propelled Baudrillard into a North American renown which eclipsed that of any of the other imported French theorists, and which continued throughout the 1980s. He was also becoming famous in the UK, Japan and Australia (which he first visited in 1984).[27] In France his notoriety had only increased with the publication in 1985 of his book *The Divine Left*, which chronicled the coming to power of François Mitterrand – the first left-wing President of the Fifth Republic – and explained how the French left had become so seduced by power it was now nothing other than a simulacrum. In the United States, his books were having to be reprinted again and again each year. He was repeatedly quoted (usually in relation to simulation and hyperreality) in the *New York Times* and *Village Voice*. He was elected to the editorial board of the influential monthly journal *Artforum*. Baudrillard did not recall being officially invited but was happy enough for his name to appear on the publication's masthead (perhaps appreciating the journal's gesture as the kind of symbolic provocation he himself was drawn to).[28] In 1985 he was commissioned to write the catalogue essay for a Barbara Kruger exhibition held from 2 to 30 May 1987 at the Mary Boone/Michael Werner Gallery in New York. He wrote that Kruger's art – her distinctive black-and-white photographs with declarative messages imposed upon them (such as 'I shop therefore I am') – could be seen 'either as advertising, pure and simple, as advertising images that are almost superficial and stereotypical, or as quasi-primitive masks that . . . perform a kind of exorcism on our society'.[29]

The apogee of Baudrillard's 'New York glory' as reluctant patron of the U.S. art scene came in March 1987 when he was invited to give the prestigious lecture on American Art and Culture at the Whitney Museum of American Art in New York.[30] Thousands clamoured for tickets, and the event was sold out months in advance. Capitalizing on the hype, the influential New York curators Tricia Collins and Richard Milazzo organized an 'Anti-Baudrillard Show' to run simultaneously at the White Columns art space in the city. Forty artists participated, though most of them were objecting not to Baudrillard but to the assumption, based on a misreading of his notion of simulation, that there was no 'real'. This had had the effect, the anti-Baudrillardians thought, of convincing theorists and practitioners there was no point in making their work political. Not surprisingly, Baudrillard professed himself to be on the side of the anti-Baudrillardians.

He fuelled the anti-Baudrillard sentiment, in any case, by using the Whitney lecture, 'Simulation and Transaesthetics: Towards the Vanishing Point of Art', to argue that contemporary art was staging its own disappearance by becoming a commodity. He also declared that 'There can't be any Simulationist school, because the simulacrum cannot be represented. This is a complete misunderstanding of what I wrote.'[31] The Simulationists were applying a concept that could not be applied. Many New York artists who had acknowledged Baudrillard's influence considered this rejection a betrayal, and art publications reported the response as such. But another way of understanding this is to regard it as an instance of Baudrillard staging his own disappearance. It was he who had written *Simulations*. There was no doubt he was interested in art, as the essay on Calle and the introduction to the Kruger volume demonstrated. But when legions of readers and art practitioners responded enthusiastically to the book, he withdrew, informed them they were misunderstood, and attempted to depart from the scene. The problem with treating Baudrillard's observations as incantations or dicta, as part of a manifesto, was that it missed his irony, his own faith in reversibility – not to mention, as Kraus later noted, an understanding of 'his modesty, humor, and politics'.[32]

In 1986 Baudrillard insisted on passing his *habilitation à diriger des recherches*. The *habilitation* is a diploma French academics must obtain in order to move up from the rank of *Maître de conférences* to that of *Professeur des Universités*. As with the doctoral thesis, candidates must produce an original research manuscript that is evaluated by a jury who decide if the student is worthy of the degree. This move seems a surprising one given Baudrillard's renown as a philosopher. He did not need an additional diploma nor enhanced academic status to give free rein to the development of his thought. Was he pressured internally at Nanterre to take this degree? Was it a kind of revenge on the academic world that he had hated so much and from which he wanted to get away at all costs? Or was it a paradoxical desire to receive the stamp of academic approval of his work, for this thinker who was now famous throughout the world? It has been suggested – just as plausibly as any of these possibilities – that Baudrillard's decision to attain 'the crowning achievement of a French university career' at this particular moment, when he was already successful and was ready to leave Nanterre for good, was precisely because he 'could not care less'. It was a perverse way of undermining the academic support he had been given.[33]

Whatever the precise motivation behind it, the text Baudrillard submitted for his *habilitation* was a dazzlingly original piece of writing, one that stands apart in his own body of work, never mind from the kind of fare normally produced for higher degrees. It was examined at the Sorbonne by a jury made up of the 'pillars' of Paris sociology at the time, 'all the stars': Eugène Enriquez, Pierre Ansart, Georges Balandier and Alain Touraine.[34] It was published as a book in France in 1987 with the title *L'Autre par lui-même* and in translation in 1988 as *The Ecstasy of Communication* as part of the 'Foreign Agents' series.

The Ecstasy of Communication is a kind of distilled guide to the most radical ideas developed by Baudrillard over the previous two decades. It is presented in the form of a Borgesian conceit that the author is an imaginary traveller who has come across these writings as if they were a forgotten manuscript and who, in the absence of supporting documents, endeavours to reconstruct the society they describe. The MIT Press (who later became the distributor for much of the Semiotext(e) list) describes it as an 'anti-manifesto', 'a mid-career assessment' that looks both forward and backwards; it portrays an 'obscene' world 'where sexuality has been superseded by pornography, knowledge by information, hysteria by schizophrenia, subject by object, and violence by terror'.[35]

The Ecstasy of Communication is one of Baudrillard's most prophetic texts, valuable even now, more than thirty years after its publication, as a key to understanding our 'permanently online, permanently connected' world.[36] This place – the world of the late 1980s and, to a different degree, the world now – is one where 'the scene and the mirror have given way to a screen and a network.' It is a place where the 'the smooth and operational surface of communication' has triumphed over transcendence or depth: 'In the image of television, the most beautiful prototypical object of this new era, the surrounding universe and our very bodies are becoming monitoring screens.'[37] It is hard not to relate the following lines to the kind of spectacle we are now confronted with every day, deep into the twenty-first century, of passers-by riveted by the enticements of their smartphone:

> Private telematics: each individual sees himself [*sic*] promoted to the controls of a hypothetical machine, isolated in a position of perfect sovereignty, at an infinite distance from his original universe; that is to say, in the same position as the astronaut in his bubble, existing in a state of weightlessness which compels the individual to remain in perpetual orbital flight, and to maintain sufficient speed in zero gravity to avoid crashing into his planet of origin.[38]

Needless to say, Baudrillard's *habilitation* was successful. Yet it did not amount to a rehabilitation, neither to Nanterre nor even to France. *The Ecstasy of Communication* was the prelude to Baudrillard leaving academia for good. While he remained physically living in Paris, in 1986 he published an exhilarating meditation on his imaginary alternative 'home', *America*. It was the first of his books in the mature phase of his writing not to be a work of theory, and would become one of his most celebrated. It paved the way for the emergence of 'other Baudrillards' who explored unusual ways of thinking and writing, new ways of capturing the world. From this point on Baudrillard would become more nomadic, bold and confident, in a way that perfectly suited the tenor of his theory and his prose.

5

'My own strange world': Baudrillard's Alternative 1980s

Ah, the desert. There was something I experienced intensely. But then all the rest is justified, since it only takes one passion to justify an existence. But that's just it – it was a passion for emptiness.[1]

Interviewer: 'If someone said, "You are a strange theorist", would that mean that there's some connection between your strange theories and your strange photographs?'
Jean Baudrillard: 'Yes, yes, exactly!'[2]

In 1987 Baudrillard announced in an interview that 'I've just left Nanterre, certain I'll never return.' His departure had been a long time coming. His almost twenty-year service had been based on a kind of uneasy equilibrium: 'I didn't have any direct participation in the administration of the university, with all the consequences for one's career that that entails, but on the other hand I had total freedom, once I'd delivered my teaching, to write, travel and do other things.' As each new book had appeared in the 1980s it confirmed he occupied a position outside conventional sociology and even philosophy, making his official university position increasingly incongruous. Moreover, in his last years at Nanterre Baudrillard felt as if he was talking to himself rather than to his students, who he thought had no interest in theory, and were 'absolutely alien' to him.[3]

He would later insist he should have left years before, but admitted he was not convinced about his appetite for doing so and even – a more mundane but serious matter – the potential he had for finding an academic post elsewhere.[4] But in 1987 it was finally the time to cut ties: 'I went over to the other side. There was a change of image, accompanied by a change of audience.'[5] That year Baudrillard did in fact join the research centre of another university, Paris Dauphine University, and stayed there until 1990. But from 1987, to all intents and purposes, he had ceased to be an academic.

The break involved a new kind of connection with theory. Baudrillard was always a fluid, energetic writer, but in his late career he would develop a new confidence in his writing, and began to write in new forms. In 1987 he began a decade-long stint as a regular contributor to the French daily newspaper *Libération*, commenting on social and cultural events. But his books *America* (1986) and *Cool Memories* (1987) were different kinds of texts altogether. Baudrillard's theory had always largely resisted academic conventions such as including endnotes, quotations and references. But these books deploy a purer style of fragmentary, aphoristic, more poetic writing. Neither could be called a work of theory.

He had begun to keep a journal early in the 1980s. Indeed *Fatal Strategies* had begun life as a project that was to combine theoretical passages and journal entries, perhaps even on the recto and verso pages of a single volume. This partly explains the feeling picked up on by some readers that, with this book more than his previous ones, Baudrillard's 'life had gone into it a bit'.[6] He found writing the journal a more pleasurable experience than the theory. But when working on the theoretical sections he found that he could no longer write the journal, as if the two projects demanded to be kept separate. The theory component did indeed become the finished version of *Fatal Strategies*, published in 1983. Yet he persisted in writing the journal in the background for enjoyment. Eventually, in 1987, it was published as the first volume of *Cool Memories: 1980–1985*. A further four *Cool Memories* volumes would appear, concluding with the fifth in the series – *2000–2004* – in 2005. In a sense these books *are* the kind of blended theory and personal observation Baudrillard originally planned for *Fatal Strategies*, only merged together, into fragments of prose.

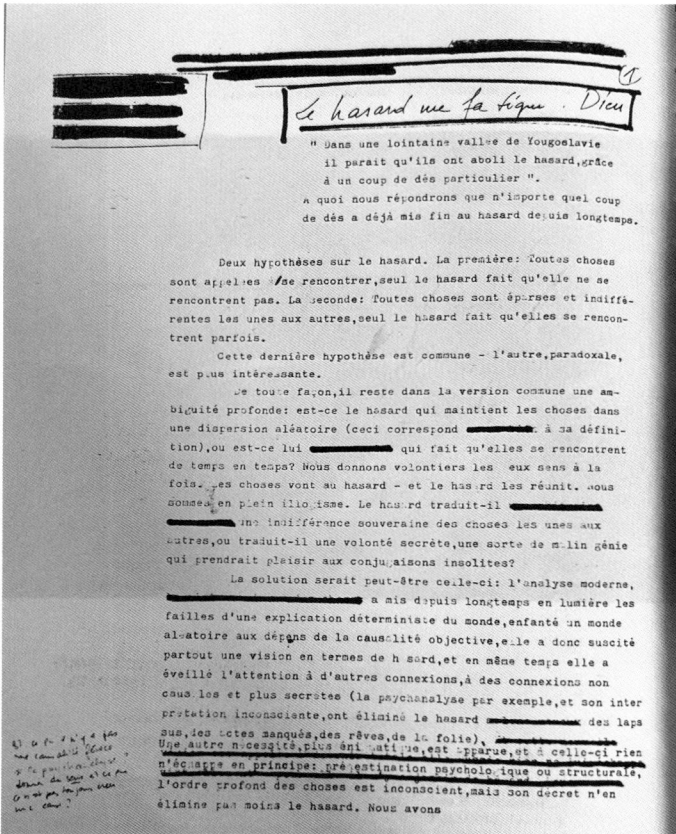

He thought, he planned, and then he wrote, with little editing or revision. Manuscript of *Cool Memories* (the note at the top of the page translates as 'I am fed up with chance. God').

The 1980s was also when Baudrillard began to take photography seriously. It was an activity he practised enthusiastically and with considerable talent. By the end of the decade, his photography created a less high-profile but equally fulfilling career for him. His photography would be exhibited many times during his lifetime – and still is today, all over the world. He saw the different activities as entirely separate, and never considered himself a 'professional' photographer to any degree. Yet photography complemented his theory, offering him another way to reflect – and reflect on – the society he explored in his books.

In fact, considered together, *America*, the *Cool Memories* series and his photography were a vital part of Baudrillard's intellectual journey in the 1980s. As he said in 1991, 'The photo and travel, because at one time they went together, the fragment, the notebook and the diary; all these functioned together as one whole, a machine with differential axles.'[7] These excursions into different forms of representation were not simply side projects. His determination to capture the world through fragments and snapshots, rather than fully fledged logical analyses, further developed his approach to theory. They also provide enticing views into his own biography and personality, albeit in a way which – typical of Baudrillard – remains mysterious and elliptical. They are at once deeply personal and yet never close to anything like a conventional autobiographical project.

America was originally a fragment of the *Cool Memories* journals that Baudrillard took out and transformed into a book of its own. When he was asked about its genesis, he would answer that *America* had been germinating for years before it was eventually published. It was mostly inspired by his trips to the United States throughout the 1970s and '80s, especially to California. When it was published in France in 1986, he said of his visits to California:

> I have experimented with every formula: the great trip through every desert, travelling 8,000 or 10,000 kilometres; three-month stays in San Diego or Los Angeles, where I was teaching, working in seminars, and then, I was walking all over of course. Or I would do a tour around conference visits, eight days here, eight days there. I have experimented with every formula, but I was not following a plan or a programme, it just happened like this over the years. I probably went

there ten or twelve times. The arrangement of the book is not chronological. The desert that you can find in the end was actually the initial desert.[8]

It is not inaccurate to describe *America* as a work of travel writing, for it reflects an actual experience, a meandering journey undertaken by the author across years and across spaces. Baudrillard wanted to rely on 'another mode of writing that is more homogeneous with American space', a way of matching style and theory, so that the reader became immersed in the book and in America, too.[9] He observed that Americans 'live in reality as if it was kind of a travelling', and so the book was constructed to be itself the product of what he thought of as 'pure travelling'.[10] This meant moving – 'horizontally', ideally at speed, as if driving or surfing – across the American landscapes and cityscapes and their sensations rather than venturing 'vertically' into its depths. This suited Baudrillard's personality, which was given to doing things speedily, as Marine Baudrillard noted: 'driving, thinking, reacting, everything'.[11] His 'hunting grounds' for gaining knowledge about America were decidedly not the libraries, lecture halls or official gatherings typically frequented by intellectuals, but 'the deserts, the mountains, Los Angeles, the freeways, the Safeways, the ghost towns, or the downtowns'.[12] The experience of America struck Baudrillard as horizontal and cinematic, and so the book needed to be horizontal and cinematic too.

Although not a scholarly work, *America*'s conceptual journey is pleasingly familiar to readers already versed in Baudrillardian ideas – and seemed to be to Baudrillard himself, too. He commented that he found in the American country and culture 'every theme I had approached in my previous books . . . suddenly and concretely unfolding in front of me'.[13] In this book, he 'walks around old concepts: seduction, simulation, fascination, fatal strategies'.[14] Discovering a reality that reflects his own theory is a quintessentially Baudrillardian move. Ludovic Leonelli has argued that 'Baudrillard does not go towards the event, but he brings it back to himself, he bends it to his own concepts.'[15]

The desert is both starting point and destination for Baudrillard's depiction of America. It is where the book begins and ends. He loved the desert more than any other part of America. 'Its emptiness suited him perfectly,' wrote Chris Kraus in 2018.[16] It was the ultimate object, in terms of Baudrillardian theory; indifferent to the subject, with a kind of agency all of its own. As he writes in *America*,

> The silence of the desert is a visual thing, too. A product of the gaze that stares out and finds nothing to reflect it. There can be no silence up in the mountains, since their very contours roar. And for there to be silence, time itself has to attain a sort of horizontality; there has to be no echo of time in the future, but simply a sliding of geological strata one upon the other giving out nothing more than a fossil murmur.[17]

He pictured the desert as the alternative to 'social and cultural America'.[18] It is an empty territory that signifies 'absolute freedom' and meaninglessness. Yet this ensures that it actually casts a powerful light on everything else about America, precisely because it is the alternative to modernity's endless social and cultural processes of imposing meaning on the world. The desert encapsulates Baudrillard's very idea of simulation, in other words.

In America, Baudrillard encountered a civilization close to 'vanishing point', where things unfold as pure fiction, where the question of being real or not real was not relevant anymore because everything was closer to hyperreality. This is what he calls in the book 'utopia achieved': 'America is neither dream nor reality. It is a hyperreality. It is a hyperreality because it is a Utopia which has behaved from the very beginning as though it were already achieved.'[19] Simulation had reached its height. In America, Baudrillard observed, 'You wonder whether the world itself isn't just here to serve as advertising copy in some other world.'[20] He found it fascinating, in his teaching or when talking about the book, that whenever he tried to explain simulation to Americans, his initial expectation that they would understand the concept better than anyone, precisely because their country was

Californian desert, by Baudrillard: 'The silence of the desert is a visual thing.'

'the paradise of simulation', turned out to be quite mistaken.
'In fact, the Americans I was dealing with did not understand
anything of it.'[21] This reinforced the value of adopting the outsider's
perspective. The outsider can defamiliarize what those who live
somewhere permanently tend to take for granted. 'I know the
deserts, their deserts, better than they do,' he wrote about the
Americans, 'since they turn their backs on their own space as the
Greeks turned their backs on the sea.'[22]

Media and screens feature repeatedly throughout *America*.
Televisions are omnipresent in the cities and motels Baudrillard
visits. Everything in the United States seemed to him to be already
on screen: 'things seem to be made of a more unreal substance;
they seem to turn and move in a void as if by a special lighting
effect, a fine membrane you pass through without noticing it.'[23]
The desert was like a western set; cities were screens 'of signs and
formulas': 'It is the same feeling you get when you step out of an
Italian or a Dutch gallery into a city that seems the very reflection
of the paintings you have just seen, as if the city had come out of the
paintings and not the other way about.'[24]

America's deserts and screens embody what Baudrillard thought of as 'astral' America. Above anything else, both conveyed a sense of emptiness. One of the memorable defamiliarizations of American life Baudrillard produces in the book is the desolate, beautiful image of a 'TV set left on in an empty room'. He marvelled at how often he witnessed this, in empty houses or hotels. 'Suddenly the TV reveals itself for what it really is: a video of another world, ultimately addressed to no one at all, delivering its images indifferently, indifferent to its own messages (you can easily imagine it still functioning after humanity has disappeared).'[25] This image, Baudrillard thought, speaks to the abstraction of a world which lives in a kind of phantasmal reflection of itself. What America actually is or is not does not matter. It is the reflection that counts. Signs are everywhere in America, but they stand in for the real.

The writing in *America* is arresting, humorous and often poetic. Nevertheless, when the English version appeared in 1988 (rendered beautifully by Chris Turner, who would become the translator of many of Baudrillard's books from this point on), it was met with puzzlement and disapproval by many American reviewers. Baudrillard was surprised by the negative response to the book.

Despite his love for the United States, and although the writing is characteristically ironic and mischievous, *America* can come across as a withering criticism of its subject. Removed from the context of Baudrillard's ideas, certain judgements were liable to cause offence, such as his observations that in America 'things almost seem endowed with a certain indulgence towards their own banality', that the country is 'the only remaining primitive society' and that 'Americans may have no identity . . . but they do have wonderful teeth.'[26] Despite the fact that he did not see the book as part of the classic 'European-writer-in-America' tradition, Baudrillard would later acknowledge that *America* is indeed a 'European book'.[27] It depicts America, more or less explicitly, as a counter-model of Europe, and this was often the source of reviewers' scorn.

Diane Rubenstein has explained that 'a reader who wishes to understand *America* should remember its construction as fiction.'[28]

Baudrillard himself suggested that '*America* should not be read in a realistic way.' Like all his books, it was really a 'scenario'.[29] After all, the clue is in the title: the book is 'America', a constructed, defamiliarized America; it is not designed to be a simulacrum. It is not the place to find interrogations of racial, gender or class injustices in the United States. These are not Baudrillard's subjects in the book, though some critics thought they ought to have been. The book's core ambiguity – that it is a fiction which needs to be understood as such in order to get to the truth – means that it illustrates Baudrillard's deliberately contradictory posture as a thinker. He is revealing something about our world, but not in the conventional academic manner. His theories do not offer to solve cryptic paradoxes; they provide a paradoxical reading of the world. As the reception to *America* showed, this posture was often misinterpreted, even among academics, and not just in France.

Baudrillard felt that the negative reception to the book in the United States was partly due to its aphoristic style:

> Aphoristic writing has no true legitimacy. It's recognized in France because it has a literary history to it, but it isn't in America! When the Americans read *America*, they reacted very badly. Writing of that kind seemed to them the work of the devil, being a sacrilege against the canonical form of the well-argued essay. They are, in fact, right in this, and that's the whole point of it.[30]

In his mind, writing aphoristically was a weapon. It allowed him to stay moored to the margins of thinking. Mike Gane has described this mission: 'In order to counter the hegemony of the system it is necessary to break out of system thinking itself, break out of thinking that is dominated by the idea of working progressively towards a final end.'[31]

The *Cool Memories* series, the most enigmatic of all Jean Baudrillard's publications, deploys the same elliptical form as *America*, but its prose is even more mysterious. The fragments – Baudrillard's thoughts and observations – are briefer, and readers have no unifying theme they can invoke to make sense of them, as they can with *America*. The thoughts leapfrog over each other. The topics are infinitely plural. What unites them is their condensed form, their elliptical, ironic, poetic tone, and the apparent disorganization. Each *Cool Memories* volume can be skimmed, or started on any page. In their aphoristic form, they reflect Baudrillard's paradoxical perception of the world. The fragment conveys 'the desire to slim things down as much as possible. At that point, you no longer grasp the same things; objects are transformed when you see them in detail, in a kind of elliptical void.'[32] The volumes also display Baudrillard's inexhaustible capacity to repeat himself, to hammer home his ideas. Few thinkers were so capable of imposing their worldview by exploring the same things over and over again in a different way. As much as anything, *Cool Memories* is a testament to Baudrillard's obsessive nature.

Baudrillard's title, *Cool Memories* – in English from the start – is mysterious in itself. In his mature work the opposition between what is 'cool' and what is 'hot' is a flexible, enigmatic pairing, used in a variety of ways. Cool stands for what neutralizes, is processed, is lacking in vitality, while 'hot' is explosive, full of unchecked energy. In other works he drew on this opposition, comparing, for example, 'hot, sexual obscenity' with 'cool communicational obscenity', or characterizing television as hot when it conveys endless information, and cool in the way it neutralizes meaning.[33] The pairing is especially enigmatic when it comes to his own notebooks. The title *Cool Memories* actually makes 'hot' memories implicit, but these are barely present and never to be indulged. Baudrillard was always suspicious of the kind of actions that could result from 'hot' feelings or memories, just as he was always suspicious of sentimentality.

Those parts of *Cool Memories* that are clearly actual memories tend to be presented as if he is separated from the warm vitality of his earlier life by the very temporal distance and the process of representation: 'It was as though I were lodged deep inside my own eye, all consciousness snuffed out, watching [memories] pass by from a great distance through its vitreous humour, its veil of boredom and déjà-vu.'[34] At one point in the first *Cool Memories* volume Baudrillard returns to the Berlin Wall, in October 1983, thirty years after his first visit. But he finds it 'impossible to feel the thrill of terror. Everything is meaningless . . . I gaze in stupefaction at this wall and cannot summon anything from my memory.'[35] Even though his early experiences in Germany were important to his development as a thinker, the experience of returning remains cool. The sensation of stasis works at both a personal and historical level. Visiting the wall is felt as an encounter with 'cold' history, where once it had been 'hot' – the same process, it is implied, Baudrillard had undergone in relation to his own past.

But most of the entries in *Cool Memories* cannot reasonably be classified as personal memories. Each volume is filled with often dissociated lines, notes, poetical snippets, dream narratives, desires, fantasies, speculations, bits of political commentary, passages of travel writing. Richard J. Lane describes these elements as 'situations', 'thought experiments', or in Baudrillard's own words as 'microscopic ideas' that are the products of 'cerebral electricity'.[36] They remain enigmatic, conveying a sense of value which remains secret, as in the following fragment: 'Life in itself is not to be despaired of; it is only mildly melancholic. Something diffuse in the daylight, something impalpable as language, gives things an air of melancholy which comes from much further back than our unconsciouses or personal histories.'[37]

The melancholic air carries across the volumes. Is Baudrillard referring to himself when he reflects that 'thinking becomes a meteorological precipitation of cerebral particles: rain and snow at the heart of the depression'?[38] We suspect that the mood of melancholia is his own disposition, but we cannot be sure. He was always adamant that he was 'not there in psychological terms' in *Cool Memories*: 'I'm not telling my own story in the episodes that come over . . . Justifying something by lived experience is weak.'[39] Perhaps he was protesting too much.

However psychologically insightful its content actually was, *Cool Memories* enabled him to veer even closer to the edge when it came to provocation and taboo. The first two volumes in particular are punctuated by fragments about seducing women, or contemplating women's bodies, youth and beauty, or pondering the differences between men and women. It is difficult to find much depth in such lines. Baudrillard is again in places prone to misogynist, even macho, thinking when it comes to the question of gender, at times expressed aggressively. He is an uncategorizable writer, but this dimension of *Cool Memories* places him in the company of outdated misogynist thinkers. Women and so-called 'feminine values' are reduced to attributes of seduction, domination and feverishness.

> The end of utopias means the end of masculine utopias, they say, leaving the way free for feminine utopias. But are there any feminine utopias? It is that naive creature, man, who exudes utopias, one of these being, precisely, woman. The latter, being a living utopia, has no need to produce any. Just as she has little reason to be fetishistic, being herself the ideal fetish.[40]

As with *Seduction* Baudrillard tried to defend himself from accusations of misogyny by pointing to the irony that was the dominant mode for his thought. Ambivalence was his way of moving forward, of producing new ideas and exploring a fresh way of writing. But it also provided him with cover, a kind of convenient shield of impunity when it came to his most provocative formulations. The poetic textuality of the *Cool Memories* series enabled him to go even further in this respect. The more detached he became from the norms of academic or philosophical writing, the more the rules of the game became his own, and the less he could be accused of breaking the rules or cheating. 'Can one enter into a dialogue with Jean Baudrillard?', Leonelli asked rhetorically.[41] Aphoristic writing meant he could blur the tracks, and drape himself in a veil of enigma.

The *Cool Memories* series provided Baudrillard with a liberating alternative to theory. Appearing every five years or so over two decades, each volume seemed to function as a kind of valve, allowing him to let off steam through a freer form of written expression. The books were still disciplined in their economy and mystery, however, and also allowed him to explore something that went to the heart of his philosophical activity: the value of focusing on detail rather than trying to grasp a sense of the whole. In one of his last works, *The Intelligence of Evil, or The Lucidity Pact*, Baudrillard wrote:

> The secret of the world is in the detail, in the fragment, in the aphorism – in the literal sense, *aphorizein* meaning to isolate, to separate, to cut off – not in the whole. It is through the detail that the anamorphosis, the metamorphosis of forms, passes, whereas the whole short-circuits this becoming by totalization of the meaning or the structure.[42]

In one of the essays included in the collection of his photographic work published in 1999, *Photographies 1985–1998*, he uses a similar formulation to describe the appeal of photography: 'looked at in general, from the angle of meaning, the world is distinctly disappointing. In detail, taken unawares, it is always perfectly self-evident.'[43]

It seems logical that a thinker so fascinated by the concept of images would create images himself. He first took up photography when the hosts of a conference in Japan – perhaps in Kyoto, in 1981 – presented him with a miniature camera as a gift. As he began to photograph more and more, he thought of himself as neither artist nor photographer but a 'maker of images' that were intended to make the world more unintelligible.[44] In the distinctive terms of his theory, photography belonged to the order of seduction. It enabled Baudrillard to discover and to foster what he considered a secret complicity with the world in a way which complemented his philosophical ambition to examine the primacy of object over subject, to trace its agency and seductive power. According to Baudrillard – and contrary to the received wisdom about the form – photographs effect the total disappearance of the subject. In photography the world thinks us, the object sees us and thinks us; it *wants* to be captured by the photographer.

Baudrillard's photographs are initially distinctive for what they do not include. He was uninterested in capturing individuals, animals, events or dramatic or violent scenes – anything that would provide an 'aura' of personal feeling, either issuing from subject or photographer. He usually resisted giving his photographs titles for the same reason, apart from the year and the name of the place they were taken. They tend to feature natural objects like trees or water, parts of a wider landscape, or depict solitary or abandoned human-made objects such as buildings, cars or streets. All are defamiliarized because of the choice of perspective – an object often appears through a close-up or as a fragment of a wider view – or the peculiar effects of the light on colour. He insisted repeatedly that he did not care whether anyone found his images beautiful. 'What interests me', he said, 'is this cry of the object at evening in the depths of the darkroom.'[45]

The impression they give is of a world emptied of people, of objects revealed in all their strangeness. They seem to be looking at us just as the viewers of the photographers are looking at them. The title of one of his essays in his 1999 collection of photographs is 'It is the Object which Thinks Us . . . '.[46] Baudrillard's best known, and most reproduced, photographs include: *Paris, 1985*, which depicts a soft object, perhaps a sofa, wrapped in a blue curtain in front of a darker blue wall; *Sainte Beuve, 1987*, an armchair draped in a deep red velvet sheet; *Saint Clément, 1987*, an old car submerged in water; or *Rio, 1996*, what appears to be a swimming pool.

It is impossible to dissociate Baudrillard's own photography from his ideas about the proliferation of images in the contemporary world. Considered side by side his art and his theory reveal how paradoxical Baudrillard's relationship to images actually was, how torn he was between an absolute captivation by images and an impulse to condemn the very idea of the image. He felt that 'the world is basically a wonderful visual report.'[47] But in his philosophy images are responsible for short-circuiting the world, destroying it in their very pretence at reproducing it. This explains the title of the lecture Baudrillard gave at the University of Sydney on 25 July 1984: 'The Evil Demon of Images'. There he argued that

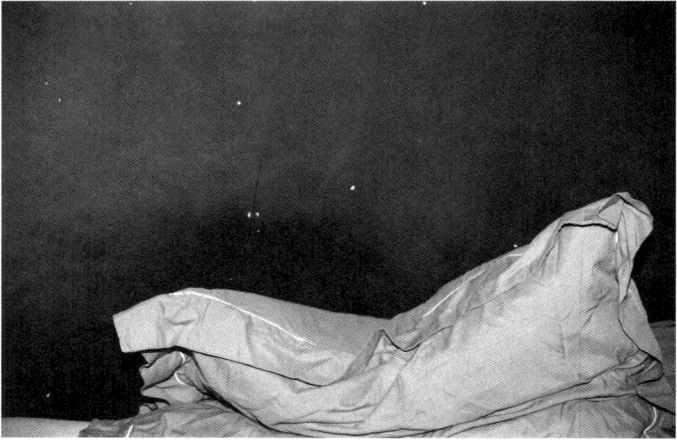

Baudrillard, *Paris, 1985*, photograph.

'by an irresistible epidemic process which no one today can control, our world has become truly infinite or rather exponential by means of images.'[48] Video and digital technology have multiplied the production and circulation of images, and, in turn, increased our fascination in them. Not only are images more present, but they are more 'full' or 'obscene', a term which, in the Baudrillardian vocabulary, means that images leave nothing hidden, retain no mystery and are too visible. This is at the heart of the problem of simulation in contemporary society. Images only pretend to look like the world, to represent it. In fact they progressively contaminate the real by creating reality. They model it, distort it, appropriate it for their own ends and, finally, they 'anticipate' reality 'to the point that the real no longer has time to be produced as such'.[49] Images anticipate reality and events, and 'it becomes impossible to tell which is the effect of the other.'[50]

Artistic photography, for Baudrillard, is actually the opposite of this visual universe, because in that art form, mystery is preserved. In fact, he contended that photography did not belong to the realm of aesthetics at all, but was more of a trompe-l'œil: 'it is an indistinctive, irreducible form, closer to the origin of representation . . . and hence opposed to any realist vision.'[51] The photographic image is able to 'exorcise' us from simulation society.[52] He insisted on the 'silence' of photographs. Whereas images in other media (such as cinema or television) ask that viewers stay silent, photographs remain silent themselves, keeping their secrets. What he loved about photography – and managed to achieve in many of his own images – was its ability to convey 'the idea of a silent apparition'.[53]

Baudrillard's art first appeared in public as part of the Venice Biennale in 1993 when a series of twenty framed photographs were displayed under the title 'Ultimate Paradox'. This was followed by the first major international solo exhibition, at the Institute of Modern Art in Brisbane between 15 July and 14 August 1994, titled 'Jean Baudrillard: The Ecstasy of Photography'. Exhibitions that followed included Austria in 1999, Paris in 2001, Moscow in 2002 and Germany in 2004.[54] Viewing the Brisbane exhibition, Baudrillard's feelings were mixed. Collected together, his photographs struck him as more aesthetic, more beautiful than he had intended. The ambivalence of his response to the image was crystallized by this experience. Photography counters simulation,

Baudrillard, *Saint Clément, 1987*, photograph. 'What interests me is this cry of the object at evening in the depths of the darkroom.'

Baudrillard, *Corbières, 1999*, photograph.

but can also be absorbed into the art system which imposes a meaning upon it.

Publicly displaying his art brought out another inescapable contradiction. As much as he wanted his photographs to evidence how the object seduced photographer and viewer, the role of the photographer – that is, Baudrillard himself – was inevitably referenced whenever they were viewed. In photography, as in all arts, the artist is unavoidably and at least implicitly present: as viewer, as selector of the image, or, in a work like *Sainte Beuve, 1987* (which perhaps has a veiled autobiographical significance as its title is that of the Paris street upon which he and Marine lived), as someone who is fond of, has covered, vacated or is about to sit on the chair in the photograph. The effect was magnified when it came to a thinker famous for his theories of the image. Baudrillard recognized as much, acknowledging that seeing his photographs on display together made him 'conscious of building a new vision of my own strange world'.[55]

Baudrillard made one exception to his policy of not featuring identifiable individuals in his photographs. *Corbières, 1999* is a veiled self-portrait taken in front of a mirror and captures Baudrillard himself in the act of taking the picture. But the camera hides his face, and the room is in near-darkness. The image captures the moment the flash operates, causing strips of fiery red light to criss-cross the photographer's shirtless torso, and the lens of the camera to resemble the irrepressible gaze of a monstrous eye: the evil demon of images himself, momentarily exposed, before disappearing again.

6

Total Freedom, 1990–2004

> I no longer take a position as an intellectual. My work now is to
> make things appear or disappear.[1]

In the 1990s and 2000s Baudrillard was able to live his dream of
'total freedom', working 'on the fringes of the systems',[2] writing
what he wanted when he wanted, analysing events, producing
writing that was itself a fatal strategy. The books he produced
throughout this period have a good claim to be considered his
best: *The Transparency of Evil* (1990), *The Illusion of the End* (1992),
The Perfect Crime (1995), *Impossible Exchange* (1999), *Telemorphosis*
(2001), *The Spirit of Terrorism* (2002) and *The Intelligence of Evil*
(2004). He thought of them as a cycle of 'theory-fictions'.[3] He
wanted these books to be read as excursions into a new terrain
for thought – away from conventional philosophy. Faced with an
enigmatic world, he felt – as he put it in a Wellek Library Lecture
in 1999 – the writer's task was not simply to 're-problematize' all
the old solutions but to use his writing 'to help to hold the world
in enigmatic tension'.[4] He thought of their style as 'splintered':
'Each fragment, each opuscule appears and disappears at the same
time. But even then they echo each other.'[5] Although book-length,
each was a collection of thematically related chapters; there was
no progressive synthesis of ideas, no patiently developed overall
thesis. The ideas are profound and worthy of analysis, but the *effect*
of Baudrillard's mature style is just as important. When reading his
books, Marine Baudrillard would occasionally wonder 'What is he
talking about?', before reasoning that 'it is not at all what he talks

about, it is the form of his thought that is imprinted in your brain and that motivates you.'[6]

In this mature phase of his writing, Baudrillard continued his practice of working very quickly, without preparatory notes. Everything was already in his mind. Essays were completed in a single stint, and he was able to work solidly for long stretches, writing sometimes for as many as ten hours without a break (and with few distractions, such as music). Editing was kept to a minimum. On re-reading a finished piece he would take some lines out, but he never added anything. Being free of the commitments of a university position meant he was able to write when he liked rather than keeping to a set routine. Despite his concentrated method of writing, however, Marine recalls that he was always ready to drop things at a moment's notice, if she suggested going out, or if they decided on a whim to take a trip or go on holiday. 'He never told me: "No, I have to work, I have to finish something."' To his mind, he was never working. She thought this was evidence of a subtle element of vanity that infused his sense of himself as writer: 'he did not like to see the effort in the things he did, for him it was vulgar to show the effort. So I never saw him work hard.'[7]

The guiding principle throughout Baudrillard's theory-fictions of the 1990s remained that of simulation, or what he began to call 'integral' or 'operational' reality: 'the perpetrating on the world of an unlimited operational project whereby everything becomes real, everything becomes visible and transparent, everything is "liberated", everything comes to fruition and has a meaning'.[8] He continued his habit of restlessly redescribing his thinking in new ways, refreshing his philosophy with terms such as the viral, evil, lucidity, the necro, impossible exchange and telemorphosis. These were linked to the enduring concepts that had structured his thinking in the previous decade: seduction, the fatal strategy, destiny, reversibility. Baudrillard, who had been a translator and poet before he was a philosopher, loved the fact that words had a life of their own. Re-labelling a concept invigorated it by revealing it from a different vantage point. All words were in fact 'passwords', enabling access to other spheres of thinking.

Jean Baudrillard at home in Paris, 1988.

But he also felt his vocabulary *needed* to be renewed. As he surveyed the world in the 1990s, he considered everything more volatile, accelerating towards the point of implosion. Systems were moving beyond their end, passing from growth to outgrowth and from movement and change to stasis, then ex-stasis (ecstasy) and metastasis. Everything was reaching critical mass, marked by excess, hypertrophy, proliferation, chain reaction. Every institutional reality had been reduced to simulation as a hyperreal version replaced it. This state of affairs was evidenced by the emergence of increasing examples of what Baudrillard considered 'extreme phenomena', events or situations which pushed categories to such an extreme (a term originally meaning 'ex-terminus', outside the limits) that they became unbalanced. Obesity collapsed the category of the body. Porn did the same to the category 'sex', just as terrorism did to violence, and, of course, the hyperreal did to the real. The Gulf War, which began in the summer of 1990, did the same to war.

Faced with such extremity, the question for Baudrillard was: what do we do now? What now, when the relentless process that defined modernity, of 'transcribing all that was of the order of the imaginary, the dream, the ideal and utopia into technical and operational reality', was complete?[9] What do we do in a situation where we can no longer use our earlier categories of rational or dialectical thought to comprehend what is happening? Or, to use the more evocative phrase he often favoured at this time (and had first used in *America*): '"What are you doing after the orgy?" What do you do when everything is available – sex, flowers, the stereotypes of life and death? This is America's problem and, through America, it has become the whole world's problem.'[10] Pondering life after the orgy is one of those analogies Baudrillard would defend as being purely illustrative, but it cannot be divested of exploitative connotations. Worse, when explaining it he sometimes envisaged the question being posed by a man to a young woman. Nevertheless Baudrillard's writing in the 1990s and 2000s is very much his attempt to write 'after the orgy' on his terms, using the weapon he was supremely equipped to use, his own *écriture*, to challenge the logic of the system.

His 1990 book *The Transparency of Evil* was written from this imagined position. It is one of his most important publications. Both terms in its title pick up ideas that had preoccupied him throughout the 1970s and early 1980s. Now, however, he was able to explore them further by applying them to contemporary 'extreme phenomena'. The book covers many of these: celebrity, drugs, disease, religious fanaticism, Holocaust denial, Michael Jackson, La Cicciolina. Like transparency, the French word *transparence* denotes a transparent quality: when something can be seen through. Yet Baudrillard gives it the sense of agency possessed by the related term *transparaître*, that which is 'capable of showing through'. Transparency is therefore the condition where everything has to be visible – not in a Foucauldian sense where visibility is the outcome of panoptic scrutiny, which brings everything into the light, but because of the complete absence of secrecy. Everything in the world is capable both of seeing through and being seen through.

Baudrillard's use of the term 'evil' – which had first featured in his writing in *Fatal Strategies* – is not to be confused with any religious understanding of this term. For him, evil was neither moral category nor theological principle. What he meant by it was more in tune with the tradition of 'dark writers' from Sade to Nietzsche. Evil is something that can radically contradict the operationalization of the world. It is 'a metaphor for a twisting of things, for a perversion of things . . . or seduction of things'.[11]

Baudrillard actually wished he had called the book *The Transparition of Evil*. 'Trans-apparition' was his neologism for evil as a ghostly form which sees and passes through what are understood as stable entities. This was his chief subject in the book: how categories, spheres, systems, disciplines have broken down and were overlapping and undercutting others, so that 'every individual category is subject to contamination, substitution is possible between any sphere and any other: there is a total confusion of types.'[12] The book uses the prefix 'trans' to single out formerly distinct categories that have been undone by this confusion. Transsexuality denotes the destabilizing of the conventional categories of male and female, transeconomics is where the economic and the political are no longer distinct, and transaesthetics is where the boundaries between art and non-art have collapsed.

Baudrillard's convictions about the undoing of social categories by extreme phenomena were strengthened by what he saw happening in the global historical arena. The geo-cultural division between Western and Eastern Europe, which had structured European life since the Second World War, broke down suddenly and completely in the early 1990s, even though the reasons behind the rupture could be traced back many years previously. Over a period of just nineteen months in 1990–91, fifteen member states of the Soviet Union declared independence. Baudrillard thought the end had been hastened by two momentous, iconic events occurring at the end of the 1980s: the Chornobyl nuclear disaster in Ukraine (then part of the USSR) in 1986, and the fall of the Berlin Wall in 1989. As much as they heralded the end of the Soviet Union, perhaps even the demise of communism as a viable system, he felt that both events also exposed the myth of a hermetically sealed West.

The demise of the Berlin Wall was a prime example of what he called the 'event strike': a world-scale event but one that did nothing to challenge the pre-eminence of globalization.[13] The Baudrillardian definition of 'event' was something that challenged the prevailing modern order. But in the 1990s it was as if meaningful events were on strike. The collapse of communism, he thought, came entirely without liberatory consequences. The Soviet empire simply entered self-destruct mode, leaving behind an empty space, like the implosion of a building. In other words, the collapse did nothing to extinguish the worst aspects of communist society that had marked the later Soviet years. Baudrillard thought these were released, like the radiation at Chornobyl, to infect the West. The West had fuelled the demise of the communist system by exporting its technologies and markets. In return the East had imposed its pollution, corruption and angst.[14]

The ultimate event strike was just on the horizon. The Gulf War lasted from 2 August 1990 to 28 February 1991, and involved an armed campaign waged by a military coalition of 35 countries led by the United States to liberate the Gulf state Kuwait following its invasion by neighbouring Iraq. The overwhelming firepower at the allied forces' disposal meant that the campaign appeared to protestors as not really a war but an act of extreme violence. In just two months the air offensive against Iraq used more high explosives than the entire allied air offensive during the Second World War.[15] There were few American casualties, and Western media seemed to care little about the number of dead and injured Iraqis.

Baudrillard was especially enraged by a double-page spread in *Libération* in early 1991 that outlined the 'pros and cons' of the war. He felt this was a 'funeral plaque' for French thought. On the face of it, it was an attempt to 'affect' the world, to display a moral conscience, yet in fact it simply justified the violence. A *Libération* contributor himself, Baudrillard published three separate articles in the newspaper in response: 'The Gulf War Will Not Take Place' (4 January 1991), 'Is the Gulf War Really Taking Place?' (6 February 1991) and 'The Gulf War Did Not Take Place' (29 March 1991). These provocative titles, redolent of Situationist slogans, drew inspiration from J. G. Ballard's 1990 novel *War Fever* in which a Third World War takes place without anyone knowing it.[16] The essays were subsequently published together in book form as *La Guerre du Golfe n'a pas eu lieu* by Éditions Galilée in May 1991.[17]

To a degree the Gulf War was like any war in the terrible destruction it wreaked on cities and communities and the devastating loss of lives it incurred, both military and civilian. Some images capturing the devastation were released, such as, most harrowingly, those detailing the carnage involving hundreds of vehicles and bodies on Highway 80 north of Al Jahra and on the coastal road to Basra on the night of 26 February 1991 (which has become one of the definitive tragic images of not only the Gulf War but all wars). Yet this war was unlike any previous one because it was the first time media images of conflict appeared on TV screens 'live' from the battlefront. It involved an unprecedented degree of control by the U.S. military over what was reported and which images were shown. The United States had learned from the chaos of the media response to the Vietnam War and so the strategy was to present what was referred to as a 'clean war', prioritizing the images of weaponry, especially footage from 'smart bombs'. These metaphors implied that casualties were somehow avoided due to the pinpoint precision of attacking specific non-human targets. Media coverage of the war was an early example of the 24-hour-news phenomenon which would gradually take hold in the 1990s, and the liberation of Kuwait was experienced by viewers across the world as a kind of live-streamed 'movie', a broadcast of instant history. The media were clearly playing the role of self-appointed brokers of reality. As a result, the Gulf War set the pattern for future mediatized events.

This explains why Baudrillard's sequence of statements – the Gulf War will not happen, is not happening, did not happen – recalled the scene in Bertolt Brecht's *Refugee Conversations*, one of his favourite references to explain simulation, where the character Ziffel reasons that 'This beer isn't a beer, but that is compensated for by the fact that this cigar isn't a cigar either. If this beer wasn't a beer and this cigar really was a cigar, then that would be a problem.'[18] To Baudrillard, the Gulf War was not a war, but this was balanced out by the fact that the news wasn't news either. The war, in reality an atrocity, and one that did nothing to disturb the dominant globalized order, was the definitive Baudrillardian 'non-event'. Because it was entirely predicted, produced, simulated, and its outcome was entirely what was intended, Baudrillard felt the only appropriate response was one which adopted the logic of the fatal strategy: 'If the war doesn't go to extremes, then writing must be allowed to, one way or another.'[19]

The anti-war sentiment underlying Baudrillard's series of essays was in tune with the many worldwide public protests against the war. Yet their titles underline the appeal of his favoured role as provocateur (or even as *eiron*, or trickster). What made them especially provocative is that as much as Baudrillard was challenging and condemning the dominant order, he steadfastly resisted the obvious liberal framing of his argument in expressions of outrage and compassion for those killed. His interventions remained characteristically 'cool'. His analysis, appearing at the height of hostilities which involved substantial human casualties, duly triggered a storm of objections by readers, journalists and academics, for its apparent nihilistic irresponsibility. Perhaps the most influential critique was by the British philosopher Christopher Norris, who mounted a case for Baudrillard as the worst example of an irresponsible trend in contemporary theory for 'uncritical theory'.[20]

Privately, Baudrillard was appalled by the war. What was happening in Iraq, he felt, was 'vile', 'enough to drive you either into depression or a rage!'[21] Yet he was determined to avoid publicly adopting the 'depressive position' which he thought was all too readily assumed by fellow intellectuals – even Paul Virilio, his friend and a philosopher he admired – in their interventions into contemporary debate. They were given to moralizing and indulging in a sentimental, ideological mode of pathos they pretended was realism but was in fact 'petitioning'. Baudrillard felt he had to choose an alternative to expressing his personal feelings on the war, to avoid the trap of the depressive position. 'If I fall into the real, I experience the same anger as the others,' he said.[22] Instead he stayed true to his long-held conviction that he would discipline himself simply to explore how things appeared, to grasp the illusion of things. As he stated later, 'I am against ethical positions in general.'[23]

The global notoriety that greeted his Gulf War interventions meant that despite – or because of – his determination to remain on the fringes of systems, Baudrillard began to feature even more prominently and widely in the cultural consciousness. He was a regular presence in newspapers and style magazines, interviewed about his theories or invited to comment on cultural affairs. As with the art scene in the 1980s, his writing was lauded by some for its visionary, up-to-the-minute manifesto-like quality, and condemned by others for its caprice and apparent lack of political conviction. In 1994 he recalled watching a French TV documentary, *Bosna!*, made by one of the darlings of French philosophy, Bernard-Henri Lévy, about the carnage in Sarajevo during the Bosnian War of 1992–5. Lévy interviewed a Sarajevo resident who told him, 'I wish Baudrillard were here to see what transparency really is.' Baudrillard greatly appreciated this, countering the resident's irony with irony of his own, praising her understanding of the term 'trans-apparition of evil'.[24] He dealt with such portrayals of himself and his ideas as phlegmatically as ever, and was especially wary of playing up to the kind of 'idolatry' he remembered being directed towards Foucault and Lacan in the 1980s, which resembled the deification of rock stars. With rock stars, he thought, at least you got the concerts and the music. 'But when you see some intellectuals fawning over the ageing, silent Lacan, that was getting absurd,' he said.[25]

Baudrillard had always been willing to give in-depth interviews. A substantial body of transcribed interviews exists, providing a valuable contribution to his thought which is more extensive than that which supplements the work of perhaps any other contemporary thinker. Throughout the 1990s and 2000s requests for interviews multiplied. The interview format suited Baudrillard. He was always supremely articulate, giving the impression that his responses had all been worked out beforehand, though in reality this was a manifestation of his remarkable ability to speak 'without a trace of hesitation', as Marine had put it.[26] The late-phase Baudrillard writes and speaks in the same way. He was gracious towards would-be interviewers, acknowledging that interviews were an obligation that came with being in the public sphere. Some got angry when he refused an invitation, as if he had a responsibility that it was their job to enforce. But he would indulge journalists and their questions patiently, maintaining a good humour, pointing out what he felt were misinterpretations or defensive over-interpretations.

Yet while he was generous to interviewers, he nevertheless preferred meeting at cafés (a particular favourite of his was Le Select in Montparnasse, once frequented by Hemingway, Picasso and Baldwin) rather than at home, so he was able to end the interview and leave when he wanted. He found interviews exhausting and, in the 1990s, felt at times like a hostage to his own work. Many interviewers, especially those from the news media, came to meet him without having read his books, or wanted simply to recreate in their finished piece a facsimile of the already known Baudrillard, trying to get him to repeat what they had read in other interviews, or to cut up his ideas and reproduce them as soundbites. His generosity created a potential trap. Unlike Foucault and Derrida, who were more protective of their legacies and would insist on reading the transcripts of interviews before publication, often rewriting them, Baudrillard favoured 'live' comment. It fitted in, after all, with his view of writing and thinking as prospective rather than retrospective and considered. He tended to leave the responsibility for editing and presenting his words to the interviewer. Inevitably, upon publication, he was shocked to read how some interviewers had presented his responses.

In 1994 he and Marine married. Baudrillard had resolved not to get married again after his first experience, so this was a momentous outcome. She felt it had taken her 'twenty years to seduce Jean, to be with me until the end'.[27] They celebrated with a party in a café on the Petite Ceinture, an abandoned nineteenth-century railway line that used to run round Paris and was at that time beginning to be repurposed for more creative pursuits.

They continued to live a contented life in Montparnasse. Unless they were travelling, they did not see many people, but settled into a comfortable pattern of working and leisure. Baudrillard enjoyed playing table tennis. He would read, and go and watch the sunset. At weekends, they would go on bike rides in the Forêt de Compiègne about 80 kilometres (50 mi.) north of Paris, where they had a small house. Although he tended to think and write at speed, he was given to moderation in most things, including drinking. He would watch TV (especially cycling, which he loved) and listen to the radio, though not much. The exception was when he got behind the wheel of his car (an Alfa Romeo: always the outsider-insider, he drove Italian cars). 'He had an incredible mastery of himself,' Marine recalled, 'except in the car.' Driving with him was a frightening experience, involving 'a total change of personality'.[28] Her solution was to have a drink and sit in the back seat while the car hurtled forward.

The simple rhythm of this Parisian existence was in striking contrast to the global turmoil that Baudrillard surveyed each day through the media, and analysed in his writing. In the mid-1990s he was preoccupied with the relation between politics and history. One effect of the collapse of communism, he argued, was the 'democratic rewriting' of the history of the West. It was the political equivalent of cosmetic surgery or stain removal.[29] Conditions were such at the end of the twentieth century that there seemed to be an urgent need to get as close as possible to each significant 'real' historical moment, to represent it and understand it. Everyone was busy revising history, putting the balance straight, determined to finish the job before the end of the century.

His 1992 book, *The Illusion of the End*, is an in-depth exploration of this millennial anxiety about the end of history. It received a great deal of commentary, partly because of the reverberations of his Gulf War commentary, but also because his declaration of 'The End of History' seemed to be a counterpart to the widely covered (and media-friendly) ideas of the conservative philosopher Francis Fukuyama, whose *The End of History and the Last Man* appeared in the same year, 1992. Baudrillard took pains to distinguish his ideas from Fukuyama's. If history had resolved all its contradictions, as Fukuyama was arguing, then surely this was optimistic? Baudrillard was tracing something more complex and disturbing altogether: the dissolution of history *as event*. What passed for history now, he maintained, was a form of interminable historicizing, or 'retrospective bookkeeping'.[30]

One of the most widely read essays in *The Illusion of the End* was 'Pataphysics of the Year 2000', a piece which repeated the Brechtian beer-is-not-a-beer formulation of his analysis of the Gulf War in its insistence that 'the year 2000 will not take place.' Throughout the 1990s – to an extent hard to fathom decades later – popular discourse was saturated with apprehension about the end of the millennium, an event known at the time via its shorthand code, Y2K. There were widespread fears that the electronic infrastructure upon which civilization was by then dependent had not factored in the prospect that the millennium's 'resetting' of history to year 00 could cause computers to be confused between the year 2000 and 1900, and cease to function reliably, resulting in such apocalyptic consequences as planes falling out of the sky. This hysterical 'party at the end of the world' mood went hand in hand in millennial culture with the urge to replay history as a kind of reckoning rather than analyse it responsibly.

In retrospect, Baudrillard's preoccupation showed that he too had succumbed to millennialism. Yet his point was that the very anticipation of Y2K meant we were already effectively existing in the year 2000. Our sense of temporality had shifted from understanding time as counted up from a point of origin to being counted down towards an endpoint. The world no longer had a history. Instead it had a destiny. This explained the cultural anxiety about the 'unresolved' problems of history and the impossibility of predicting the future: 'We can see everything and when we can see everything we can't *foresee* anything,' he said.[31] The anxiety was encapsulated above all, and humorously, for Baudrillard, by the huge digital clock that had been installed in 1989 on the piazza in front of the Centre Pompidou at Beaubourg and was counting down the seconds one by one until midnight on 31 December 1999. It was removed after a few years, presumably, he reasoned, because of the fears about the potentially dangerous social consequences created by the spectacle, as if a bomb would go off to signal the end of the world when the countdown got to zero. Even more hilarious to him was his discovery that the displaced clock had not been dismantled nor switched off, but stored at the back of a warehouse in the Parc de la Villette where it continued its countdown – only unobserved, in the corner of a cellar in the dark. Its replacement was a noticeboard placed beside the Eiffel Tower which more reassuringly counted down the time remaining in terms not of seconds but of days, a less worryingly instantaneous unit of time.

It became something of a commonplace in the 1990s to accuse Baudrillard of lacking political commitment or, worse, being a reactionary. The view came mainly from a Marxist position (exemplified by his influential American champion and critic the cultural theorist Douglas Kellner). Baudrillard rejected the criticism, reasoning that it was founded upon an old-fashioned and in fact conservative understanding of the social. He remained scornful of the moral petitioning his intellectual contemporaries pretended was true political engagement. He kept up a 'position of incredulity' which contrasted with their sentimental posture.[32] 'I still feel responsibility at an individual level,' he once said, but 'I don't think an intellectual can speak for anything or anyone.'[33] In 1994 he criticized the American cultural critic Susan Sontag's staging of Samuel Beckett's *Waiting for Godot* in a besieged Sarajevo during the Bosnian War a year before, because he felt it was an example of unintentional imperialism which chimed with George H. W. Bush's contemporaneous, politically charged, notion of a 'New World Order'.[34] Sontag responded by calling Baudrillard 'a political idiot. Maybe a moral idiot too.'[35] Baudrillard was happy to acknowledge that it was true he no longer had a political 'position', and stated this was because his stance was that of his preferred fantasy-exemplar, the peasant. 'An indocile person', he said, 'is one who refuses to be educated, in other words, to get involved with the world of signs.'[36]

The 1990s zeal for the kind of 'necrospective' post-historical mourning explored in *The Transparency of Evil* and *The Illusion of the End* had a deleterious effect on meaningful political intervention. The West was faced with problems which were becoming more catastrophic – war, terrorism, famine. Yet rather than attempting to solve these real-world problems it was choosing to go backwards, to try to 'clean up' history retrospectively, correct all the errors, account for the violence and create a utopia. The millenarian anxieties about history also explained why the dominant affect driving political sentiment was hate. But it was a hatred different from the kind – such as class war – that had fuelled previous political moments. This one did not have a fixed object. Hate was being directed at more general things, such as politics itself, manifested as a hatred for the 'political class'. It was visible, for example, in the various political scandals surrounding the Mitterrand government in the 1990s, such as the 'Angolagate' secret arms sales scandal, or the Elf–Dumas big business lobbying affair.[37] Essentially hate was an expression of frustration at the fact there was 'no possible resolution to all the problems posed by history', leading to 'a rejection of the course of history' itself.[38]

In the early 1990s Baudrillard had begun using a new metaphor which brought together the themes of his previous work but which lent itself especially well to 'theory-fiction': 'the perfect crime'. He published a book with this title in 1995. Its backdrop is the post-communist 1990s, in which the world has become 'characterized by intensified globalization – of technologies, the market, tourism, information – and by the predominance of "universality", of values, human rights, freedoms, culture, democracy'.[39] For Baudrillard, however, this represented no liberal utopia, but a triumph for the overall production and operationalization of the real. The outcome was that otherness was eliminated, everything rendered the same. This was what the book described as the perfect crime – 'the murder of reality'. But like any supposedly perfect crime in a detective thriller the extermination of the world is not undetectable, and Baudrillard – so the conceit framing the book goes – positions himself as metaphysical detective. The criminals, that is, the perpetrators of simulation, 'leave traces everywhere – viruses, lapses, germs, catastrophes – signs of defect, or imperfection, which are like our species' signature in the heart of an artificial world'.[40] *The Perfect Crime* tracks down these traces.

There is more than a touch of humour in this detective-story scenario. Yet, it was not unusual for 'the ironic premise at the heart' of Baudrillard's work, as Chris Kraus described it, to be missed by critics.[41] Subtle self-deprecation was also a consistent feature of his response to his increased celebrity in the latter half of the 1990s. In 1996 he featured in an advertising campaign for the furniture brand Vitra, reclining on a designer swivel chair in a photo taken by Swiss photographer Christian Coigny. As Ludovic Leonelli observed, the image conveyed to its viewers a message which echoed that of his earlier book, *The Consumer Society*:

> All of this does not matter . . . You know very well that the system plays endlessly with signs, digests and recycles everything, and first and foremost that which contests it . . . There is no escape . . . The only solution is to adopt a distanced and amused position and, if possible, for oneself to become a sign.[42]

According to those who knew him best, this self-deprecating attitude was in keeping with his natural humility. Marine Baudrillard recalls that he was never two-faced or hypocritical, always calm and non-judgemental and seldom angry: 'If he met the President of the Republic it was exactly the same as when he spoke with the porter.' The only exceptions were if some 'imbecile' driver got it his way, or if someone asked him a stupid question at a conference or a dinner.[43]

An attitude of quizzical self-deprecation was central to Baudrillard's participation in the 'Chance: Three Days in the Desert' festival held at a casino in Primm, Nevada, in November 1996, organized by Kraus. She conceived of an ambitious gathering that would bring together a diverse community of people seeking inspiration from art, music and philosophy, and facilitate chance encounters with others. Poets, students, dancers and musicians would party with croupiers, stockbrokers and land rights activists (the casino was on Native American land, on the California–Nevada state line).[44] Baudrillard was to be the star attraction. But Kraus wanted to honour rather than deify him, and envisaged the event as

'Chance is a special effect that redeems the paradoxical nature of our lives': Whiskey Pete's Casino in Nevada, venue for the Chance Event, 1996.

a living and breathing manifesto spearheaded by him rather than a conventional academic conference devoted to his work. He provided her with a tagline for the event, to help promote it: 'Chance is a special effect that redeems the paradoxical nature of our lives.'[45]

The event was co-headlined by the transgender performance-theorist Sandy Stone, who gave the main address on the first night – accompanied by a rendition of a Cole Porter parody, 'I Get a Kick Out of Jean B'. The eclectic bill included a keynote address in the form of a trip-hop set by New York DJ Paul D. Miller, a.k.a. DJ Spooky, readings by the poet Diane di Prima and her partner Sheppard Powell, an I-Ching diviner, and introductions to chaos theory delivered by a Wall Street trader and a rollerblading mathematician. Side sessions included the Mexican poet Luis Bauz performing a tribute to Baudrillard. Marine Baudrillard remembers robots walking around. There was a Sunday morning walk at dawn in the desert outside the casino.

Baudrillard's lecture was scheduled for the Saturday night on the main stage in the casino's black box theatre. Delivered in English, it was entitled 'Towards an End with Freedom, or How Not to Escape Your Destiny, or the Fatal versus the Fractal, or This World We Think', though it also had a number of other lengthy subtitles.[46] Lotringer stayed up to the small hours of Saturday morning translating it, and Baudrillard was still editing it right up to the last minute. The talk was a typically profound piece of theoretical speculation, but Baudrillard gauged the spirit of the event and played up to it. He had been persuaded by Lotringer and Marine to don a gold lamé tuxedo with mirror lapels which the singer Amy Stoll had driven to Las Vegas to rent. By the time he took the stage – introduced as the 'sultan of simulation'[47] – it was 2 a.m., and 'the theatre looked like an enormous slumber party, with people lying on the theatre floor and gazing at the ceiling'. 'No one understood a word' of his lecture, Kraus remembers, 'but it didn't matter.'[48] When he had finished, the 'Chance Band' joined him on the stage and improvised as he reprised passages from his talk and read a poem he had written in the 1980s, 'Motel-Suicide', with its catchy refrain 'suicide . . . suicide moi'.

Baudrillard, *Las Vegas, 1996*, photograph.

Baudrillard's fears that he would never be forgiven for the gold tuxedo proved accurate. The following weekend the event was front-page news in the *Los Angeles Times*, complete with a photo of him in the gold jacket on stage at the microphone, while Stoll looked on in her cocktail-waitress outfit. For all the event's inclusivity, energy and irreverence, the reception from the mainstream art community in the United States was predictably stuffy. It did not help that his essay 'The Conspiracy of Art' had appeared a few months earlier (in May 1996, in *Libération*), reiterating the argument in *The Transparency of Evil* about how the 'transaestheticization' of the whole of society meant that art itself had become 'nullified'.[49] An *Artforum* review of the event mocked it for its pretentiousness, and the way it exemplified the 'unspoken trend in academia towards transforming the professor of theory into the rock star'. The article did concede, however, that Baudrillard 'brought off this divine visitation with some measure of panache'.[50]

Baudrillard's notion of simulation received its most wide-ranging global publicity when it featured in *The Matrix* (1999), by the

Wachowski siblings. The film is a variation on the invasion-of-the-body-snatchers narrative in science fiction. It is about a programmer, Thomas Anderson, or 'Neo', who is drawn into a battle against a powerful computer network which has constructed the reality that envelops everyone on Earth via a system called the Matrix. Early on there is a scene where Neo conceals money and computer disks inside a volume of *Simulacra and Simulation*. We see it open at 'On Nihilism', the last essay in Baudrillard's book. The invitation to read the film in terms of a popularized version of his theory of simulation is clear. In fact the original intention was for the film to be even more explicit about its inspiration. Earlier drafts of the screenplay have the freedom-fighter Morpheus telling Neo, 'As in Baudrillard's vision, your whole life has been spent inside the map not the territory.'[51]

Something about Baudrillard's work had appealed to readers and producers of science fiction since the 1980s. In 1993 he had been asked to contribute to an Oliver Stone sci-fi TV drama series entitled *Wild Palms*, about 'a virtual-reality magnate who seized power using "holograms" he controlled'.[52] He had declined. But he was amused at featuring now in a Hollywood film, especially one he thought was actually quite good. *The Matrix* represented more or less accurately his notion of simulation, conveying how the real itself is generated by preceding models, the effect this has on one's sense of individual identity, and how humanity needs to recognize and rebel against this 'crime'. Another of the film's freedom-fighters, Cypher, says at one point: 'You know . . . I know this steak doesn't exist. I know that when I put it in my mouth the Matrix is telling my brain that it is juicy and delicious. After nine years, you know what I realize? Ignorance is bliss.'

But Baudrillard thought *The Matrix* made an 'embarrassing error' in choosing to show the contrast between simulated reality and the real. In the film, he declared, 'Everything belonging to the order of dream, utopia and phantasm is given expression, "realized".'[53] The 'desert of the real' – a phrase from *Simulacra and Simulation* – is presented as a decaying, apocalyptic image of Chicago, in other words the territory the map falsifies (as a result of the projections of the 'neuro-interactive simulation' that is the Matrix).

Baudrillard turned down offers to act as a 'theoretical consultant' for the two sequels to *The Matrix*, *The Matrix Reloaded* and *The Matrix Revolutions* (both 2003), as he felt it would be precisely the kind of thing which 'professionalised' him.[54] Yet the success of *The Matrix* – as well as other films released around the turn of the millennium that seemed designed to be explained in the terms of his theory of simulation, such as *The Truman Show*, *eXistenZ*, *Minority Report* and *Mulholland Drive* – meant that in 1999 Baudrillard had reached a global audience outside academia which was unsurpassed for any contemporary thinker. He was frustrated that this was so often due to an enthusiastic misinterpretation of his concept of simulation. A few years earlier, in 1995, his Japanese translator Fuki Tsukahara had informed him that the reason he was no longer hearing much from Japanese readers of his work, despite how widely read the translations were, was because they felt his prophecies had been realized and the world they were living in was now 'Baudrillardian'.[55]

This global interest also stirred up an old resentment. He lamented that he still was not taken seriously by French intellectuals. By 1999 he noted that there had only been one conference on his work in France, organized by friends, compared to some twenty books published on his work in English-speaking countries. That same year, the point was underlined as he was asked to deliver the prestigious annual series of Wellek Library Lectures in Critical Theory at the University of California, Irvine (which were subsequently published as *The Vital Illusion*) in which he described our situation as we approached the new millennium as 'wholly pataphysical' because 'everything around us has passed beyond its own limits, has moved beyond the laws of physics and metaphysics.'[56] In reality Baudrillard was not alone in this feeling of neglect. François Cusset has shown that the positive reception to both Derrida and Lyotard abroad was also in inverse proportion to their reputation in France. One might say the situation was similar to the establishment of film noir in the 1940s and '50s, only in reverse: the French produced French theory but the Americans invented it.

In any case, by the late 1990s a new space had been cleared for theory. The dominance of French thinkers associated with 'poststructuralism', such as Althusser, Derrida, Foucault and Lyotard, was on the wane, and a new generation of theorists, including Slavoj Žižek, Peter Sloterdijk and Giorgio Agamben, were being enthusiastically read and cited. Baudrillard admired these thinkers (he said he could 'feel' Žižek even though he completely disagreed with everything he wrote), and accepted graciously and with characteristic irony that the end of his influence, and even the end of his writing career, was looming into view.[57] After all, the choice to put on the gold lamé jacket at the Chance Event had been partly a valedictory gesture, to position Baudrillard as, in Kraus's words, an 'aging diva, the Liberace of the art world'.[58]

The metaphor used in the title of his 1997 book of interviews with Philippe Petit, *Le Paroxyste indifférent* (the English version is *Paroxysm*), sums up the valedictory spirit of much of Baudrillard's late writing: the paroxysm was 'the penultimate moment, that is to say not the final moment, but the moment just before the end, just before there's nothing more to be said'.[59] This book was followed in 1999 by another overview of his work, *Mots de passe* (Passwords), a TV documentary similar to Gilles Deleuze's *Abécédaire* (1988–9). *Passwords* – turned into a book in 2000 – offered twelve accessible entry points into Baudrillard's thinking: the object, seduction, value, impossible exchange, the obscene, the virtual, symbolic exchange, the transparency of evil, the perfect crime, destiny, duality and thought. This text, which was much more accessible than *The Ecstasy of Communication*, implied Baudrillard's thought had always been consistent, and was now worthy of retrospective analysis as much as it retained a vitality in its diagnosis of the present.

The millennium duly arrived, bringing much excitement but none of the expected technological melodrama. Jean and Marine saw in the New Year without doing anything special to mark the occasion. The mundanity of the Y2K clock simply resetting to 00 without any drama bore out Baudrillard's conviction about the continuing 'event strike'. However, it was not far into the new century when an event occurred which caused him to rethink this assumption. On 11 September 2001 terrorists flew two planes into the World Trade Center in New York, causing both Twin Towers to collapse. As horrifying as the event was, and as deeply painful as the reverberations were for so many, from the perspective of social and political theory 9/11's televisual status as spectacle made it especially suited for analysis through a Baudrillardian frame. It illustrated his point about the fragility of simulation society; that modern systems are vulnerable to being reversed or collapsed. It exemplified in particular the thesis advanced in a book which he had recently published, *Impossible Exchange* (1999), about the challenge a 'primitive' outlook posed to a modern one. This text self-consciously echoed *Symbolic Exchange and Death*, the new adjective reflecting Baudrillard's view that the kind of symbolic exchange privileged in the earlier volume was no longer viable. When every single term has an attributed and exchangeable value, exchange can no longer function because equivalence is all there is.

Baudrillard had been considering terrorism as a serious challenge to the Western system since as far back as *For a Critique of the Political Economy of the Sign* in 1972. Terrorism was not political activism, and nor was it a protest against oppression or even capitalism. There was no ideology or desired objective that could explain it – even those of a doctrine such as radical Islam. Its very senselessness was the point. This view was underlined by 9/11, which involved a different kind of terrorist act, more gruesome even than hostage-taking, the kind of violence that had typified terrorism in the late twentieth century. It involved the attackers taking civilians hostage, yet they did not use their captives to make demands, but killed them, and themselves, and many others, in the act.

On 19 February 2002 Baudrillard took part in a debate about the aftermath of 9/11, held at New York University, and broadcast on *France Culture* a few days later. His book *The Spirit of Terrorism*, published later that year as part of a Verso Books mini-series on 9/11 alongside volumes by Slavoj Žižek and Paul Virilio, contended that the atrocities confirmed that death challenged the fundamental principle behind symbolic (or impossible) exchange: the attribution of value and meaning to everything.[60] A system, Baudrillard thought, cannot be destroyed by a dialectical revolution within the terms of the system itself. The only challenge that worked was one posed in the form of 'a gift to which it cannot respond except by its own death and collapse'.[61] The attacks on the Twin Towers effectively presented the United States and the West with a singular primitive 'gift' which – as in Mauss's theory of potlatch – trapped them into responding.

Their response was to launch the 'War on Terror', and attack two Islamic countries for providing comfort to terrorists: first Afghanistan, resulting in the strongest power in the world decimating one of the weakest, and then Iraq, in an attempt to finish the job begun a decade earlier with Operation Desert Storm and rid the world of Saddam Hussein. The nearly 3,000 deaths on 11 September – in the Twin Towers attack, as well as during further attacks on the Pentagon, and on board a fourth hijacked plane, United Airlines Flight 93, which crashed into a field in Pennsylvania – were avenged by the deaths of many thousands more. The logic of potlatch dictated that the proper response, which Baudrillard of course knew was quite impossible, would have been not to retaliate, but to forgive.

Already notorious after his Gulf War interventions, Baudrillard's interpretation of 9/11 – and, again, his apparent lack of empathy for the victims – caused outrage. But his refusal to compromise his own ethics meant he again walked an uncomfortable line, given how outrageous and abhorrent to most people both events were. Terrorism, the form which emerges when no other kind of resistance seems possible, was compatible with the conviction Baudrillard had articulated so many times prior to 9/11, that a system will inevitably implode and reverse – an outcome that, in a range of different contexts, he willed to occur. After all, he had once, twenty years before, described himself as an intellectual 'terrorist'.[62]

Yet once again he brushed off the opprobrium, resolute in his determination not to compromise his writing by slipping into a sentimental or depressive intellectual position. In interviews he patiently acknowledged that he knew that there are those who committed the barbaric acts, and whom they were affiliated to; that the plane crashes were unbearably destructive; and that it would be 'idiotic' to praise murderous attacks.[63] But he refused to back away from his conviction that there was nevertheless a symbolic meaning to the catastrophe, one that went beyond any intention the attackers may have had. Challenged in particular about his view that America aroused the desire for its own destruction – in his mind, because of its incontestable status as the sole global superpower – he would reply that one must not confuse the messenger with the message.[64]

A coda to Baudrillard's analysis of 9/11 came with his interpretation, in an essay entitled 'War Porn', of the scandal surrounding the 2004 discovery of photographs from the Abu Ghraib prison in Iraq, used as a detention centre by the U.S. military during the post-9/11 American occupation. The images revealed horrific human-rights violations and war crimes perpetrated by U.S. military personnel against detainees, including physical abuse, sexual humiliation, physical and psychological torture, rape and the desecration of corpses. The scandal eventually led to prosecutions and an apology issued by President George W. Bush and his Defense Secretary Donald Rumsfeld. Taken in the very prison the Saddam Hussein regime used to torture oppressed Iraqi citizens, the horrifying sadistic sexual and physical photographs were 'pornographic' in the specifically Baudrillardian sense, too: exemplifications of the obscene. They figured as an alternative 'counter-gift' thrown back at the established order – which was humiliated by this challenge to its official narrative about the war on terror.

Both 9/11 and Abu Ghraib were examples that fitted into established Baudrillardian frames of analysis about the culture of hyperreality and obscenity. But they were also counter-examples which occasioned him to update his earlier declaration of an 'event-strike'. In 2004 he published the book he regarded as the conclusion to his cycle of 'theory-fictions', *The Intelligence of Evil, or The Lucidity Pact*. It was also a sequel of sorts to *The Transparency of Evil*, as it was presided over by the metaphor of seeing through and showing through. At this time, however, Baudrillard was conscious of writing 'in the shadow-cone' of the events of 9/11.[65] The phrase 'the lucidity pact' denoted the reversibility that had occurred following the destruction of the Twin Towers and the disturbing revelations about Abu Ghraib. Events were once again possible – or, at least, it was clear that some events could occur which were not fully knowable, operational, simulated and produced by the dominant order. Baudrillard was always comfortable revising his own previously expressed ideas, and keen to challenge himself. The final words in the book were these: 'A work, an object, a piece of architecture, a photograph, but equally a crime or an event, must: be the allegory of something, be a challenge to someone, bring chance into play and produce vertigo.'[66]

Conclusion: Beyond

Dying is nothing. You have to know how to disappear.[1]

Jean never wanted disciples, has not at all prepared his succession,
his posterity . . . never. To do this, he should have been convinced
he was in possession of a truth and that one should absolutely
protect it. No, such was not typical of Jean. He had a way to
metabolize reality, to teach us how to metabolize what happens
to us.[2]

In 2000 an interviewer referred to the ironic decade-by-decade
micro-biography Baudrillard had set out a few years earlier in
Cool Memories II ('Pataphysician at twenty – situationist at thirty
– utopian at forty – viral and metaleptic at sixty – the whole of
my history') and asked what he thought he was at age seventy.[3]
Baudrillard replied, 'I would say that I am . . . transfini. Beyond the
end. It was my fateful strategy to go beyond the concept, so as to see
what happens beyond.'[4]

Baudrillard always liked to declare endings: the end of the social,
of politics, sexuality, art, history. Death was an important trope
in his thought. The historical revisionism he had written about
in *The Transparency of Evil* and *The Illusion of the End* was part of
a 'necrological' phase he thought culture had been stuck in since
the 1980s. The central argument in *Symbolic Exchange and Death*
still underpins the late books *Impossible Exchange* and *The Spirit of
Terrorism*. Death has no value and no place in a society in which
everything is accounted for and every negative has been absorbed

into reality – in contrast to the 'primitive' counter-system in which death provides a challenge to the living.

In his last decade or so, Baudrillard turned this logic, unflinchingly, towards his own mortality. The valedictory dimension of his 1990s work (visible in the retrospective overviews *Paroxysm* and *Passwords*, or, more performatively, in the 'Liberace' suit and his rendition of 'Motel-Suicide' at the Chance Event) involved reflections in interviews on the great 1960s generation of Parisian philosophers. In 1997 he referred to the 'holocaust in just a few years of a whole generation of intellectual big names (Sartre, Barthes, Lacan, Foucault, Althusser, Deleuze, Debord)'.[5] By the early 2000s, only a few – including Derrida, Lyotard and himself – were survivors.

In summer 2004 he attended a conference in Karlsruhe, Germany, entitled 'Baudrillard and the Arts', dedicated to his work and in honour of his 75th birthday. This was more of a conventional academic conference than the Chance Event. It was conceived as a

Jean Baudrillard, in slippers and dressing gown, throwing away his post in the 1990s. Marine Baudrillard was given this image after Baudrillard's death by a photographer who had every day watched a man putting his post straight into a rubbish bin and wondered who it was, until a friend told him, 'Yes! It's Jean Baudrillard.'

major commemoration of the impact Baudrillard's thinking had had on the arts and culture, and was accompanied by an exhibition of his photographs and aphorisms. Its organizer, Peter Gente, wrote that his aim was

> to make it clear that Jean Baudrillard not only approaches the arts in a critical and interpretive way, but that he himself is also in the process of becoming an artist. One might call him an artist-philosopher and set him alongside Nietzsche, Adorno, Klossowski, Roland Barthes, Peter Weibel and others.[6]

Chris Kraus, who also spoke at the symposium, picked up on the theme, describing Baudrillard as more than just 'a narrator of concepts': 'He is a conceptual artist, a performative philosopher who realizes, in a profound, post-Brechtian way, that one speaks always through masks and [the] elusions of personae that make up what's known as identity.'[7]

The following year, 2005, Baudrillard's health took a turn for the worse as he learned the prostate cancer, which he had first suspected in 2001 (but only sought advice about years later, to pacify Marine), had spread.[8] He understood the valedictory flavour of Karlsruhe, and was gratified that the people who attended the symposium – conducted mainly in German, which he still spoke fluently – took his work so seriously (though this acknowledgement was laced with his usual irritation about how he was treated in France). He battled cancer for two more years, continuing to work and to write whenever he was able. In 2005 he delivered talks in Rio de Janeiro, Montréal, Quito and, in early November of that year, New York – making what was his last visit to the United States. The final volume of *Cool Memories* (*Cool Memories v: 2000–2004*) and an important collection of essays in English translation edited by Sylvère Lotringer, *The Conspiracy of Art* (which included two far-reaching analyses of media culture, 'Telemorphosis' and 'Dust-Breeding'), both appeared in 2005, as did a series of dialogues with the Argentinian philosopher Enrique Valiente Noailles entitled *Exiles from Dialogue* (a play on Brecht's *Flüchtlingsgespräche*, or *Refugee*

Conversations, which he had translated back in 1963). In 2006 he was involved in planning for a wall of images to be presented in the orangery in the gardens of the Château de Vendôme in the Loire Valley as part of the 'Promenades photographiques de Vendôme' event. His own photographs would eventually be exhibited there in 2017 as part of the 'Qui est photographie?' exhibition.

Another notable event in 2005 was the publication, finally, of Baudrillard's first essay, on pataphysics. It appeared without fanfare, in a limited-edition fourteen-page book-format run of only 177 numbered copies, 44 of which were signed by Baudrillard himself. Shortly afterwards a different translation featured in *The Conspiracy of Art*. 'Pataphysics' therefore became one of the last works published while Baudrillard was still alive, and brought with it the possibility, as one reviewer noted, of indulging in the pleasure of 'examining Baudrillard backwards'.[9] This first work could now be read as a lens through which one could make sense of what came after. There is an unmistakably retrospective element to this decision to publish the essay, alongside an interview with Lotringer in which he discussed it: a subtle but self-conscious effort to survey the entirety of his career. Baudrillard told Lotringer that as a young man he tried to write like Artaud but finally settled for being Baudrillard.[10]

Jean Baudrillard died on 6 March 2007. The worldwide obituaries made clear his global status as a great cultural figure, while revealing how difficult he was to place in any one category.[11] The *International Herald Tribune* quoted the French Minister of Education's declaration that France had lost one of its 'great figures of sociological thought'. The *New York Times* obituary called him a 'postmodern guru' and 'critic and provocateur'. *The Times* and the *Los Angeles Times* both referred to his influence over popular culture, artists and writers, the former publication quoting J. G. Ballard's remark that Baudrillard 'was the most important French thinker of the last twenty years'. There were also, naturally, references to some of his controversial interventions, such as his Gulf War articles, and his 1994 criticism of Susan Sontag. Just as inevitably, there were many ironic references to his most famous theory, simulation.

Baudrillard, 2001.

Publications declared 'Jean Baudrillard's Death Did Not Take Place' and 'Reality Claims Gallic Provocateur', or asked 'Has This Man Really Died?'

On the morning of his funeral, on 13 March 2007, around 150 people – family, close friends, well-wishers and devoted readers – gathered at the Cimetière du Montparnasse, a few minutes' walk from the Baudrillards' apartment on rue Sainte-Beuve. Some attendees received notification of the details by way of a card Marine had produced with Baudrillard's veiled self-portrait *Corbières, 1999*, on one side. 'I chose this picture because I thought that moment was the birth [of all], and that it was right to send the image of a navel even for death.'[12] The then French Minister of Culture Renaud Donnedieu de Vabres delivered an address, and concluded by remarking that he wished he had been able to speak to Baudrillard in person. Lotringer noted wryly that had Baudrillard been to the École normale supérieure and been appointed Chair at the Sorbonne (which he said Baudrillard had vaguely hoped to be on presenting his postdoctoral *habilitation* back in 1986), Vabres would surely already have done so. Lotringer said that in the Cimetière du Montparnasse he kept looking around, 'expecting to see him there – his stocky body, his familiar face with its large features, his eyes twinkling behind his large glasses, his head slightly bent, listening to his own eulogies with a quiet sneer'.[13] In the memorial piece he wrote soon after, Lotringer described Baudrillard as 'a historian of the future, looking back from the end of the world at contemporary society'.[14]

The news of Baudrillard's death was received by many not just as the end to his own original thinking but as the final chapter in the era he represented. *Eurozine* declared that 'Now the last of the great French philosophers of the 1970s is dead.'[15] His ability to inhabit and evade categories – artist-philosopher, critic, postmodernist, guru, provocateur, historian of the future, last great French philosopher – is perhaps why he both encapsulated and transcended this era. Jean-Michel Rabaté has insisted that theory is not a branch of philosophy. Its roots are less in specific 'schools' of thought or particular methodologies than in the critical spirit of the literary and the avant-garde, as exemplified in movements such as Surrealism; it is distinguished by its ability to 'hystericize' other thinkers or commentators, to ask difficult foundational questions, and to keep asking them.[16] If this is true, then perhaps 'theorist' remains the best designation for Jean Baudrillard – better than 'writer' or 'pataphysician' or even Jacques Donzelot's appealing term 'patasociologist'.[17] One of Baudrillard's most quoted lines is from *Impossible Exchange*: 'The world is given to us as something enigmatic and unintelligible, and the task of thought is to make it, if possible, more enigmatic and more unintelligible.'[18] Or perhaps Baudrillard represents the passing of a cultural phase which is even more difficult to define, as the media theorist Peter Lunenfeld said when thinking back on the Chance Event in 2017:

Baudrillard's grave, Cimetière du Montparnasse, named by Marine 'Le jardin des outrages'.

No one, really, has replaced Jean Baudrillard. I think it's wrong that so many people bashed younger artists for the way they appropriated Baudrillard – that's just what artists do. Artists have the right to pick up everything and use it. And Baudrillard wrote in a way that encouraged that, that encouraged a leap into the void, a willingness to go for it. He stood in for a certain moment when people read books and tried to make these books part of their lives, and that hasn't really been repeated.[19]

In the years that followed Baudrillard's death some previously unpublished work appeared. Some of it, like the book *Radical Alterity* (2008), a transcription of a seminar discussion from the early 1990s between Baudrillard and the socio-economist Marc Guillaume, was earlier work republished in book format. But there were five notable new essays, worked-up versions of the 2005 lectures Baudrillard had given in various locations. They were intended to be part of a new book, but his illness meant he was never able to complete this project. Two of these essays, 'Carnival and Cannibal' and 'Ventriloquial Evil', appeared together as *Carnival and Cannibal, or, The Play of Global Antagonism* (2008). Lotringer published the other three together in 2010 (along with a reprinted 2005 interview with the French magazine *Chronic'art*) in a short volume called *The Agony of Power*: 'From Domination to Hegemony', 'The White Terror of the World Order' and 'Where Good Grows'. This late work develops Baudrillard's ongoing analysis of 'integral reality' by considering it in an explicitly global, in places directly postcolonial, context. 'Carnival and Cannibal', for example, argues that, historically, the West has exported its economic, military, technological, religious and political values through a process of 'carnivalization', but this process generates a counter-impulse, 'cannibalization', which sees power steadily undermined and reversed by the very people it carnivalizes.

Baudrillard's final book *Why Hasn't Everything Already Disappeared?* was written in January 2007 and published – sadly and appropriately, given its title and themes – in March that year, the month of his death and funeral. It is as much of a retrospective as the more systematic *Passwords* (2000). The question posed in its title, perhaps more than any other, is the one that nagged at Baudrillard his whole life. This short book is perhaps the neatest distillation of the brilliant 'one idea' which sustained his intellectual mission.

'Why is there something rather than nothing?' is a question asked by metaphysicians since the seventeenth century, such as Spinoza, Leibniz, Wittgenstein and Heidegger. Why do things – Earth, human beings, the universe – exist at all rather than there just being nothing? Baudrillard approaches the question from the other end, as it were, as the title of his book suggests. Why has existence not lapsed into nothingness? Fittingly, it is his most metaphysical book, engaging less with 'the world' than his other late-phase writings (that is, seldom analysing social, cultural or political events), and concentrating instead on the metaphysical consequences of his thought. Its concise focus means it might also be regarded as his most personal book – personal in the special Baudrillardian sense of its author being 'in there' but to an extent which is not clear, even to himself.[20] The word 'I' features only once – apart from its opening epigraph, which reproduces, unattributed, a near-quotation from the mid-century avant-garde writer Raymond Queneau's poem 'L'Explication des métaphores':

> When I speak of time, it is not yet
> When I speak of a place, it has disappeared
> When I speak of a man, he's already dead
> When I speak of time, it already is no more[21]

In Queneau's original, the man 'will soon be dead'. *Why Hasn't Everything Already Disappeared?* reads in places as if Baudrillard is both contemplating his own imminent death, and writing *as if* already dead. But of course his desire was to disappear rather than die. Compared to death, disappearance is 'the desire no longer to be there'.[22] If we understand 'being there' as being something rather than nothing, or the situation where something or someone is present as a result of being produced and operationalized by integral reality, given a value, *simulated*, in other words, then disappearance is the desire to remove oneself from the system, like unplugging oneself from the matrix in the movie. However, disappearing does not mean simply entering another 'something', as happens in the *The Matrix*, but revealing 'the world as it is'.[23]

Throughout his work, Baudrillard's analysis of simulation society was focused on disappearance rather than death. Simulation society attributes presence, meaning, value and function to everything and in doing so eliminates mystery and nothingness. As a result the real disappears – though it leaves its traces in seduction, art and symbolic exchange, and systems can implode or reverse through their own momentum or as a result of fatal strategies. Disappearance can be deliberate or accidental, but it leaves a trace. It thereby leaves something active in place; something that can influence things. In *Why Hasn't Everything Already Disappeared?* Baudrillard again invokes one of his favourite images to describe this: the grin of the Cheshire Cat, which still hovers in the air after the rest of the cat has vanished.

'The whole art', he writes, 'is to know how to disappear before dying and instead of dying.'[24] In 1997, after a sold-out and much-hyped talk at the Institute of Contemporary Arts in London, Baudrillard told a journalist 'I am nothing.'[25] As much as this was an expression of modesty in the face of his fame, it was also a reassertion of his scepticism about identity. He disappeared into his writing. The ironic one-word summarizing of his life – pataphysician, situationist, utopian, metaleptic, 'transfini' – shows him putting this into action, as the summary causes the substance of a life to dissolve into condensed, poetic, fragments.

By going 'beyond the concept', his writing performs a disappearing act too. Even though his own conceptual apparatus was remarkably consistent throughout four decades of publishing books, going beyond the concept meant seeking details and counter-examples which exceed or elude the theoretical framework, and acknowledging that ideas can take on a life of their own. He observed in *Cool Memories IV* (a text preoccupied with what it means to go 'beyond the end') that a book was finished 'when you think you have taken it as far as you can' but nevertheless some of its readers 'will carry it to its end and beyond its end'.[26] Baudrillard insists that 'everything that disappears – institutions, values, prohibitions, ideologies, even ideas – continues to lead a clandestine existence and exert an occult influence.'[27] This is what resulted from his death, as indeed it does after the deaths of all influential thinkers. He disappeared from the cultural scene, from the world of theory. But this left the traces of his ideas. They are still active, lingering like the disembodied grin of the Cheshire Cat, or Lotringer's vision of their architect's 'quiet sneer' at his own funeral. The sociologist Jean-Louis Violeau explained Baudrillard's tendency to overindulge in proclamations of 'the end' of things, to always be 'the first to say "it's over"', as part of his commitment to writing from 'beyond'.[28] It made him a kind of ghost, always there but hard to pin down, appearing and disappearing at the same time, haunting conventional academic pretension.

A preoccupation of Baudrillard's writing over the previous decade was with the effects of digital technology. He began to document the condition we experience as our reality now. As he put it in 2001, the Internet is 'the core of the problem today'.[29] A few years before he had referred to how, these days, 'you enter your life as you would walk on to a screen. You slip on your own life like a data suit.'[30] He declared, in a play on Lacan's notion of the 'mirror stage', that humanity had entered a 'video stage' in which there was no escape from 'image-recording, sound-recording, this immediate, simultaneous consciousness-recording'. The screen had replaced the mirror because 'What we get isn't really our own image, but an instantaneous recording in real time'.[31] All this, he thought, turned social performance into an 'appearing act' which had nothing to do 'with *being* – or even with *being seen*'; it was not 'I exist, I am here!', but 'I am visible, I am an image – look! look! This is not even narcissism, merely an extraversion without depth, a sort of self-promoting ingenuousness whereby everyone becomes manager of their own appearance.'[32]

Why Hasn't Everything Already Disappeared? advances these ideas further, presenting digitization as the next decisive step in the production of 'objective' reality in its entirety, ensuring map finally covers territory, transforming everything into 'a virtual, digital, computerized, numerical reality'.[33] A logical outcome of this age of digital hegemony, he thought, was that humans were finally being expelled from the world, as if through a built-in obsolescence. In 'a perfectly objective universe . . . there is no subject any longer, there is no one there to see it. The world no longer has need of us, nor of our representation.'[34] As he observed in *Cool Memories IV*, 'the world's only extremity is the extremity of endless circulation. Wherever you are, you are hostage to the global network. It is impossible to cut the umbilical cord. You are yourself an extreme phenomenon, gone beyond your own end.'[35] All this leads Baudrillard to supplant the title of the book with another rhetorical question: 'hasn't everything already disappeared?'[36]

These may seem like pessimistic conclusions, as if this final book amounts to Baudrillard 'signing off' from his life's project. Maybe he was. Lotringer's obituary description of him as 'a historian of the future, looking back from the end of the world at contemporary society' seems especially appropriate for this last work. But *Why Hasn't Everything Already Disappeared?* also reminds us of the fragility of this global network, this powerful force, in the face of singular 'rogue events', or terrorism, or the Abu Ghraib photographs.[37] Everything that disappears or is made to disappear leaves a trace. Then there is the writing itself. Baudrillard's uniquely declarative style, its capacity to be more like a manifesto than a philosophical treatise, meant it was never just a sombre analysis of the way things were. It was a call to arms, a reminder that there is an alternative to 'integral reality'. In Marine Baudrillard's memorable phrase, his writing offers us a way to 'metabolize reality, to teach us how to metabolize what happens to us'.

Baudrillard's unique and uncompromising critical life was dedicated to writing not as a means of resistance (because he believed that direct, subversive resistance was outdated and ineffective), but as a way to construct an alternative kind of world – his 'own, strange world', with its own set of rules – which functioned as an 'obstacle' by simply existing, by being an alternative.[38] It is this need to build something different, something singular, which explains his determination to remain outside intellectual movements or academic systems, and his provocative responses to events, like the Gulf War or 9/11, or to other thinkers, such as Foucault or Sontag. He wanted to oppose the 'appearing act' which defines simulation society with his own logic of disappearance. His writing reminds those who read it that orthodoxy and power can always be countered by irony, seduction, art or surprise.

References

Introduction: The Disappearance of Jean Baudrillard

1 Jean Baudrillard, *Cool Memories IV: 1995–2000*, trans. Chris Turner (New York, 2003), p. 24.
2 Larissa MacFarquhar, 'Baudrillard on Tour', *New Yorker*, 20 November 2005, www.newyorker.com.
3 François Cusset, *French Theory: How Foucault, Derrida, Deleuze, and Co. Transformed the Intellectual Life of the United States*, trans. Jeff Fort (Minneapolis, MN, 2008), p. 4.
4 Jean Baudrillard, 'Too Bad about Patagonia', interview with Michel Jourde and Hadrien Laroche [1990], in *Jean Baudrillard: From Hyperreality to Disappearance: Uncollected Interviews*, ed. Richard G. Smith and David B. Clarke (Edinburgh, 2015), pp. 7–18 (p. 15).
5 Truls Lie and Jean Baudrillard, 'The Art of Disappearing', *Le Monde diplomatique*, 17 April 2007, www.eurozine.com.
6 Eva Wiseman, 'Sophie Calle: "What attracts me is absence, missing, death . . . "', *The Observer*, 2 July 2017, www.theguardian.com; Chris Kraus, 'This Is Chance', in *Social Practices* (South Pasadena, CA, 2018), pp. 25–40 (pp. 25–6); Cody C. Delistraty, 'Online Relationships Are Real', *The Atlantic*, 2 October 2014, www.theatlantic.com; Richard J. Lane, 'Obituary: Jean Baudrillard', *Radical Philosophy*, 144 (July/August 2007), www.radicalphilosophy.com.
7 According to Marine Baudrillard in the rare book *Baudrillard/Baudrillard*, written by Marine Baudrillard and published both in French and Chinese (Nanjing, 2012), p. 3.
8 Jean Baudrillard, *Cool Memories II: 1987–1990*, trans. Chris Turner (Durham, NC, 1996), p. 4.
9 Jean Baudrillard, *Fragments: Conversations with François L'Yvonnet*, trans. Chris Turner (London, 2004), pp. 103–4.

10   Serge Latouche, *Remember Baudrillard* (Paris, 2019), p. 45. Our
     translation; emphasis in original.
11   Gary Genosko, Introduction to Jean Baudrillard, *The Uncollected
     Baudrillard*, ed. Gary Genosko (London, 2001), pp. 1–12 (pp. 8, 1).
12   Baudrillard, *Cool Memories IV*, p. 33.
13   Chris Turner, 'The Intelligence of Evil: An Introduction', in Jean
     Baudrillard, *The Intelligence of Evil: The Lucidity Pact*, trans. Chris
     Turner (London, 2013), pp. 1–12 (p. 4). Turner is referring to
     Baudrillard's 1978 book *In the Shadow of the Silent Majorities*, trans.
     Paul Foss, Paul Patton and John Johnston (New York, 1983).
14   Jean Baudrillard, *Utopia Deferred: Writings from 'Utopie' (1967–1978)*,
     trans. Stuart Kendall (New York, 2006), p. 21.
15   '*The Matrix* Decoded: *Le Nouvel Observateur* Interview with Jean
     Baudrillard', *International Journal of Baudrillard Studies*, 1/2 (July
     2004), https://baudrillardstudies.ubishops.ca.
16   Baudrillard, *Utopia Deferred*, p. 24.
17   David Macey, 'Obituary: Jean Baudrillard', *Radical Philosophy*, 144
     (July/August 2007), pp. 61–6.
18   Kraus, 'This Is Chance', p. 28.
19   Jean Baudrillard, 'I Don't Belong to the Club, to the Seraglio', interview
     with Mike Gane and Monique Arnaud [1993], in *Baudrillard Live:
     Selected Interviews*, ed. Mike Gane (London, 1993), pp. 19–25 (p. 25).
20   Jean Baudrillard, 'Forget Artaud (Jean Baudrillard / Sylvère
     Lotringer)', in *The Conspiracy of Art*, trans. Ames Hodges (New York,
     2005), pp. 217–36 (pp. 217–18).
21   Ibid., p. 218.
22   Ibid., pp. 230–31.
23   Jean Baudrillard, 'The Transparency of Kitsch: A Conversation with
     Enrico Baj', in *The Uncollected Baudrillard*, ed. Genosko, pp. 143–54
     (p. 148).
24   Jean Baudrillard, 'Baudrillard's Seduction', interview with Patrice
     Bollon [1983], in *Baudrillard Live*, ed. Gane, pp. 36–40 (p. 38).
25   Jean Baudrillard, 'Le Mal ventriloque', in *Carnaval et cannibale* (Paris,
     2008), pp. 16–40 (p. 37). Our translation.
26   MacFarquhar, 'Baudrillard on Tour'.
27   'Jean Baudrillard, n'est plus là pour analyser notre monde. Mais
     il l'a déjà fait': 'Jean Baudrillard, l'intelligence du temps qui vient',
     International Conference, Cerisy-la-Salle, France (9–16 August 2019),
     https://cerisy-colloques.fr/baudrillard2019.
28   Cusset, *French Theory*, p. 231.

29 Tara Brabazon and Steve Redhead, 'Baudrillard in Drag: Lady
    Gaga and the Accelerated Cycles of Pop', *Americana: The Journal of
    American Popular Culture, 1900 to Present*, xii/2 (Fall 2013), www.
    americanpopularculture.com.
30 Martin Legros, '"Don't Look Up", le film qui "réalise" la prophétie de
    Baudrillard', *Philosophy Magazine*, 18 January 2022, www.philomag.com.
31 Emmanuelle Fantin and Camille Zéhenne, *Le Livre dont Jean Baudrillard
    est le héros* (Paris, 2023).
32 Jean Baudrillard, *America*, trans. Chris Turner (London, 2010), p. 39.
33 Ibid., p. 40.
34 Christa Steinle, 'Preface', in Jean Baudrillard, *Photographies 1985–1998:
    Within the Horizon of the Object: Objects in This Mirror Are Closer than
    They Appear* (Ostfildern-Ruit, 1999), pp. 16–19.

1 Belonging and Breaking Away, 1929–66

1 Jean Baudrillard, *Paroxysm: Interviews with Philippe Petit*, trans. Chris
   Turner (London and New York, 1998), p. 49.
2 Jean Baudrillard, *Cool Memories v: 2000–2004*, trans. Chris Turner
   (Oxford, 2006), pp. 107–8.
3 Jean Baudrillard, *Cool Memories iv: 1995–2000*, trans. Chris Turner
   (London, 2003), p. 67.
4 Jean Baudrillard, in Caroline Bayard and Graham Knight, 'Vivisecting
   the 90s: An Interview with Jean Baudrillard' [1995], in *Jean Baudrillard:
   From Hyperreality to Disappearance: Uncollected Interviews*, ed. Richard
   G. Smith and David B. Clarke (Edinburgh, 2015), pp. 76–94 (p. 92).
5 Jean Baudrillard, 'I Don't Belong to the Club, to the Seraglio',
   interview with Mike Gane and Monique Arnaud [1993], in *Baudrillard
   Live: Selected Interviews*, ed. Mike Gane (London, 1993), pp. 19–25
   (p. 19).
6 Jean Baudrillard, 'Fractal Theory', interview with Nicholas Zurbrugg
   [1990], in *Baudrillard Live*, ed. Gane, pp. 165–71 (p. 167).
7 Baudrillard, 'I Don't Belong to the Club, to the Seraglio', p. 25.
8 Jean Baudrillard, *Cool Memories ii: 1987–1990* (Paris, 1990), pp. 17–18.
   Our translation.
9 Marine Baudrillard, communication to the authors.
10 Jean Baudrillard, *D'un fragment l'autre: entretiens avec François L'Yvonnet*
    (Paris, 2001), p. 21. Our translation.
11 Baudrillard, *Paroxysm*, p. 49.

12 Chris Kraus, 'This Is Chance', in *Social Practices* (South Pasadena, CA, 2018), pp. 25–40 (p. 29).

13 Personal archives of Marine Baudrillard. Our translation.

14 Ibid.

15 Ibid.

16 Ibid.

17 Ibid.

18 Jean Baudrillard, 'I Like the Cinema', interview with C. Charbonnier [1982], in *Baudrillard Live*, ed. Gane, pp. 29–35 (p. 33).

19 Baudrillard, 'I Don't Belong to the Club, to the Seraglio', p. 19.

20 Jean Baudrillard, *Fragments: Conversations with François L'Yvonnet*, trans. Chris Turner (London, 2004), p. 103.

21 Personal archives of Marine Baudrillard. Our translation.

22 Ibid.

23 Baudrillard, 'I Don't Belong to the Club, to the Seraglio', p. 21.

24 Ibid., p. 19.

25 Baudrillard, *Fragments*, pp. 4–5.

26 Marine Baudrillard, communication to the authors.

27 Serge Latouche, *Remember Baudrillard* (Paris, 2019), p. 54.

28 Baudrillard's own modified definition, 'unique imaginary solutions to the absence of problems', is even better when it comes to understanding what he would seek to expose in his own writings: Jean Baudrillard, *Pataphysique* (Paris, 2005), p. 41. Our translation.

29 Alfred Jarry, *Exploits and Opinions of Dr. Faustroll, Pataphysician*, trans. Simon Watson Taylor (Boston, MA, 1996).

30 Baudrillard, *Fragments*, p. 4.

31 Dennis Duncan, 'Introduction to Le Grand Jeu', in René Daumal et al., *Theory of the Grand Game: Writings from 'Le Grand Jeu'*, ed. and trans. Dennis Duncan (London, 2015), pp. 7–28 (p. 11).

32 Jean Baudrillard, 'Forget Artaud (Jean Baudrillard / Sylvère Lotringer)', in *The Conspiracy of Art*, trans. Ames Hodges (New York, 2005), pp. 217–36 (p. 219).

33 Latouche, *Remember Baudrillard*, p. 53.

34 Jean Baudrillard, 'Pataphysics', in *The Conspiracy of Art*, trans. Hodges, pp. 213–16 (p. 214).

35 Baudrillard, *Fragments*, p. 5.

36 Ibid., p. 4.

37 Jean Baudrillard, *Cool Memories: 1980–1985*, trans. Chris Turner (London, 1990), p. 201.

38 Baudrillard, 'Forget Artaud', p. 219.

39 Ibid., pp. 235–6.
40 Ibid., p. 219.
41 Jean Baudrillard, *L'Ange de Stuc* (Paris, 1978).
42 Jean Baudrillard, *Simulations*, trans. Paul Foss, Paul Patton and Philip Beitchman (New York, 1983), p. 88.
43 Jean Baudrillard, 'Stucco Angel', trans. Sophie Thomas, in *The Uncollected Baudrillard*, ed. Gary Genosko (London, 2001), pp. 76–90 (p. 89).
44 Jean Baudrillard, 'The Politics of Seduction', interview with Suzanne Moore and Stephen Johnstone, in *Baudrillard Live*, ed. Gane, pp. 152–5 (p. 154).
45 Contradictorily, Baudrillard did later tell Sylvère Lotringer in 2005 that he was 'a Germanist by training'; Baudrillard, 'Forget Artaud', p. 218.
46 Sylvère Lotringer, 'Untimely Meditations: On Jean Baudrillard', *Artforum* (2007), https://baudrillardstudies.ubishops.ca.
47 Jean Baudrillard, 'Jean Baudrillard, "On *Utopie*"', interview with Jean-Louis Voileau, in *Utopia Deferred: Writings from 'Utopie' (1967–1978)*, trans. Stuart Kendall (New York, 2006), pp. 13–30.
48 Gary Genosko, Introduction to Baudrillard, *The Uncollected Baudrillard*, ed. Genosko, pp. 1–12 (p. 4).
49 René Burri, *Les Allemands*, ed. Jean Baudrillard (Paris, 1963).
50 Jean Baudrillard, 'This Beer Isn't a Beer', interview with Anne Laurent [1991], in *Baudrillard Live*, ed. Gane, pp. 180–90 (p. 180).
51 Jean Baudrillard, 'Germany: Is It a New World?', in *The Uncollected Baudrillard*, ed. Genosko, pp. 25–8 (p. 26).
52 Jean Baudrillard, 'Anorexic Ruins', trans. David Antal, in *Looking Back on the End of the World*, ed. Dietmar Kamper and Christoph Wulf (Cambridge, MA, 1989).
53 Baudrillard, 'I Don't Belong to the Club, to the Seraglio', p. 21.

2 Objects and Objections, 1966–70

1 Jean Baudrillard, *Fragments: Conversations with François L'Yvonnet*, trans. Chris Turner (London, 2004), p. 3.
2 François Cusset, *French Theory: How Foucault, Derrida, Deleuze, and Co. Transformed the Intellectual Life of the United States*, trans. Jeff Fort (Minneapolis, MN, 2008), p. 1.
3 Ibid., p. 69.
4 Serge Latouche, *Remember Baudrillard* (Paris, 2019), p. 58. Our translation.

5 Jean Baudrillard, 'La Sociologie et la disparition de son objet: entretien avec Henry-Pierre Jeudy', *Lignes*, special issue: 'Crise et critique de la sociologie', ed. Jean Baudrillard et al., III/38 (1999), pp. 27–39 (pp. 27–8). Our translation.

6 Neil Badmington, 'Very Fine Gifts: An Interview with Chris Turner', *Barthes Studies*, 1 (2015), pp. 158–64.

7 *Jean Baudrillard et le Centre Pompidou: une biographie intellectuelle*, ed. Valérie Guillaume (Lormont, 2013), p. 42. Our translation.

8 Guillaume, *Jean Baudrillard et le Centre Pompidou*, p. 43. Our translation.

9 Jean Baudrillard, 'Jean Baudrillard, "On *Utopie*"', interview with Jean-Louis Voileau, in *Utopia Deferred: Writings from 'Utopie' (1967–1978)*, trans. Stuart Kendall (New York, 2006), pp. 13–30 (p. 29).

10 Jean Baudrillard, 'Baudrillard: The Interview', interview with Mike Gane and Monique Arnaud [1993], in *Baudrillard Live: Selected Interviews*, ed. Mike Gane (London, 1993), pp. 199–207 (p. 204).

11 There was initial dissatisfaction when it was decreed that all students applying to study Arts at the Sorbonne who resided in areas of western Paris and in nearby suburbs had to register at Nanterre; many students found commuting to the university difficult; there were divisions among the faculty between those who were politically far-left and those who were moderate-leaning; and in March a three-day strike was organized on the campus by UNEF (Union nationale des étudiants de France), a left-wing students' union, in protest against the government's higher-education policy. See François Crouzet, 'A University Besieged: Nanterre, 1967–69', *Political Science Quarterly*, LXXXIV/2 (June 1969), pp. 328–50.

12 Simon Ridley and Paolo Stuppia, 'Activation of Student Protest: Reactions, Repression and Memory at Nanterre University, Paris 1968–2018', in *When Students Protest: Universities in the Global North*, ed. Judith Bessant, Analicia Mejia Mesinas and Sarah Pickard (London, 2021), pp. 17–32.

13 Michel Clouscard, *Néo-fascisme et idéologie du désir: genèse du libéralisme libertaire* (Paris, 2013).

14 This was expanded into a book, also called *The Right to the City*, published in 1968.

15 Baudrillard, *Fragments*, p. 15.

16 'Debord's uncompromising critiques of society, his disdain for all those who make a living within such a society . . . made him a man with few allies anywhere'; Robert Greene, Introduction to Guy Debord,

Considerations on the Assassination of Gérard Lebovici, trans. Robert Greene (Los Angeles, CA, 2001), pp. i–ix (p. iv).

17 Jean Baudrillard, *Simulacra and Simulation*, trans. Sheila Faria Glaser (Ann Arbor, MI, 1994), p. 163.

18 'De la misère en milieu étudiant, considérée sous ses aspects économique, politique, psychologique, sexuel et notamment intellectuel et de quelques moyens pour y remédier' (On the Poverty of Student Life, Considered in Its Economic, Political, Psychological, Sexual and Especially Intellectual Aspects, with a Modest Proposal for Doing Away with It) was published anonymously in 1966 in Strasbourg. It was attributed to 'members of the Situationist International and Students of Strasbourg University' but later revealed to have been written by the SI member Mustapha Khayati under Debord's direction. In *Situationist International Anthology*, ed. and trans. Ken Knabb (Berkeley, CA, 2006), pp. 408–29.

19 Situationist International, 'Our Goals and Methods in the Strasbourg Scandal', in *Situationist International Anthology*, ed. Knabb, pp. 263–72 (p. 272).

20 Jean Baudrillard, *Cool Memories II: 1987–1990*, trans. Chris Turner (Durham, NC, 1996), p. 83.

21 Baudrillard, *Simulacra and Simulation*, p. 6.

22 Debord in 1985: 'If the Situationist International still existed today, it would inevitably be called a terrorist group': Debord, *Considerations on the Assassination of Gérard Lebovici*, p. 10.

23 Gabriel Rockhill, 'The Myth of 1968 Thought and the French Intelligentsia: Historical Commodity Fetishism and Ideological Rollback', *Monthly Review: An Independent Socialist Magazine*, 1 June 2023, https://monthlyreview.org.

24 Pierre Mounier, *Pierre Bourdieu: une introduction* (Paris, 2001), p. 217.

25 Sylvère Lotringer, 'Untimely Meditations: On Jean Baudrillard', *Artforum* (2007), https://baudrillardstudies.ubishops.ca.

26 'Utopia: The Smile of the Cheshire Cat'. The original editorial statement of the *Utopie* journal, no. 4, October 1971. In Jean Baudrillard, *The Uncollected Baudrillard*, ed. Gary Genosko (London, 2001), pp. 59–60 (p. 59).

27 'Utopia: The Smile of the Cheshire Cat', p. 59. Baudrillard also draws parallels with the Cheshire's Cat's grin in, for example, *Cool Memories V* and *Impossible Exchange*: Jean Baudrillard, *Cool Memories V: 2000–2004*, trans. Chris Turner (Oxford, 2006), p. 28; Jean Baudrillard, *Impossible Exchange*, trans. Chris Turner (London, 2001), p. 55.

28   Tiphaine Samoyault, *Roland Barthes: A Biography*, trans. Andrew Brown (Cambridge, 2017), p. 244.

29   Baudrillard, *Fragments*, p. 3.

30   Jean Baudrillard, *The System of Objects*, trans. James Benedict (London, 2005), p. 1.

31   Ibid., p. 38.

32   Ibid., p. 94.

33   Ibid., p. 39.

34   Ibid., p. 180.

35   D. S. Greenberg, 'Nanterre: A Year Later at Campus Where French Student Revolt Began', *Science*, LXIV/3885 (13 June 1969), pp. 1261–4 (p. 1262).

36   Jean-Louis Violeau, 'Foreword: Baudrillard, the Ghost', in Jean Baudrillard, *The Ecstasy of Communication*, trans. Bernard Schütze and Caroline Schütze (South Pasadena, CA, 2012), pp. 9–16 (pp. 10–11).

37   George Ritzer, Introduction to Jean Baudrillard, *The Consumer Society: Myths and Structures*, trans. Chris Turner (London, 1998), pp. 1–24 (p. 18).

38   Jean Baudrillard, *The Consumer Society*, p. 25.

39   Ibid., p. 193. Emphasis in original.

40   Ibid., p. 26.

41   Ibid., p. 43.

42   Ibid., p. 43.

43   Ibid., p. 197.

44   Ibid., pp. 43–4.

45   Ibid., p. 7.

46   Martin Beck, *The Aspen Complex* (Cambridge, MA, 2012), p. 8.

47   Craig Buckley and Jean-Louis Violeau, 'Introduction: The Echo of Utopia', in *Utopie: Texts and Projects, 1967–1978*, ed. Craig Buckley and Jean-Louis Violeau, trans. Jean-Marie Clarke (Cambridge, MA, 2011), pp. 9–21 (p. 19).

48   Gilles de Bure, 'The Summits of Aspen' [1971], trans. Patricia Chen, *Rosa B*, V (2013), available at http://rosab.net/en.

49   Baudrillard, 'On *Utopie*', p. 18.

50   Ibid., p. 28.

51   Ibid., p. 13.

52   Ibid., p. 26.

53   Ibid., p. 16.

54   Ibid., p. 18.

55   Ibid., p. 27.

56 Ibid., p. 20.
57 Ibid.

3 Becoming 'Baudrillard': Seductions and Provocations, 1970–79

1 Jean Baudrillard, 'Game with Vestiges', interview with Salvatore Mele and Mark Titmarsh [1984], in *Baudrillard Live: Selected Interviews*, ed. Mike Gane (London, 1993), pp. 81–95 (p. 81). Emphasis in original.
2 Jean Baudrillard, 'Postface: Forget Baudrillard: An Interview with Sylvère Lotringer', in *Forget Foucault*, trans. Nicole Dufresne (Los Angeles, CA, 1987), pp. 71–123 (p. 85).
3 Baudrillard, 'Game with Vestiges', p. 81.
4 *Apostrophes* was a prime-time literary talk show broadcast on Friday nights on the channel Antenne 2 (subsequently France 2) that ran from 1975 to 1990. It was one of the most watched programmes on French television of this period.
5 Tomasso Fagioli, Eleonora Conciliis and Nicholas Ruiz III, 'Reinventing the Real: A Conversation with Marine Dupuis Baudrillard', *Kritikos: An International and Interdisciplinary Journal of Postmodern Cultural Sound, Text and Image*, XV (Summer 2018), https://intertheory.org/marinebaudrillard.htm.
6 Marine Baudrillard, communication to the authors.
7 Fagioli, Conciliis and Ruiz, 'Reinventing the Real'.
8 Ibid.
9 Ibid.
10 Ibid.
11 Baudrillard, 'Game with Vestiges', p. 81.
12 Jean Baudrillard, *Simulacra and Simulation*, trans. Sheila Faria Glaser (Ann Arbor, MI, 1994), p. 163.
13 Jean Baudrillard, 'Une entrevue avec Jean Baudrillard', interview by Guy Bellavance, *Parachute*, 31 (June–August 1983), pp. 26–33 (p. 32). Our translation.
14 Jean Baudrillard, 'Baudrillard's Seduction', interview with Patrice Bollon [1983], in *Baudrillard Live*, ed. Gane, pp. 36–40 (p. 39).
15 Jean Baudrillard, 'Jean Baudrillard, "On *Utopie*"', interview with Jean-Louis Voileau, in *Utopia Deferred: Writings from 'Utopie' (1967–1978)*, trans. Stuart Kendall (New York, 2006), pp. 13–30 (p. 16).
16 Fagioli, Conciliis and Ruiz, 'Reinventing the Real'.

17 Mark Poster, 'Translator's Introduction', in Jean Baudrillard, *The Mirror of Production*, trans. Mark Poster (St Louis, MO, 1975), p. 13.

18 Sylvère Lotringer, 'Introduction: Domination and Servitude', in Jean Baudrillard, *The Agony of Power*, trans. Ames Hodges (South Pasadena, CA, 2010), pp. 7–29 (p. 12); Steve Redhead, *We Have Never Been Postmodern: Theory at the Speed of Light* (Edinburgh, 2011).

19 Jean Baudrillard, *For a Critique of the Political Economy of the Sign*, trans. Charles Levin (London, 2019), p. 48.

20 Jean Baudrillard, *Symbolic Exchange and Death*, trans. Iain Hamilton Grant (London, 1993), p. 126. We are tempted to use the global COVID-19 pandemic as an example of the enduring validity of this theory. The risk and fear of death was everywhere, and millions died, but publicly and in the media, actual death was largely kept off-stage, represented mainly as statistics.

21 Mike Gane, Introduction to *Baudrillard Live*, ed. Gane, pp. 1–16 (p. 3).

22 Jean Baudrillard, *Paroxysm: Interviews with Philippe Petit*, trans. Chris Turner (London and New York, 1998), p. 79.

23 Sylvère Lotringer, 'Untimely Meditations: On Jean Baudrillard', *Artforum* (2007), https://baudrillardstudies.ubishops.ca.

24 Ibid.

25 Ibid.

26 François Cusset, *French Theory: How Foucault, Derrida, Deleuze, and Co. Transformed the Intellectual Life of the United States*, trans. Jeff Fort (Minneapolis, MN, 2008), p. 69.

27 Baudrillard, *Paroxysm*, p. 80.

28 Lotringer, 'Untimely Meditations'.

29 Baudrillard, *Paroxysm*, p. 87.

30 Ibid., pp. 79–80.

31 Baudrillard, 'On *Utopie*', p. 28.

32 Lotringer, 'Untimely Meditations'.

33 Jean Baudrillard, *America*, trans. Chris Turner (London, 2010), p. 31. Many sources document Baudrillard's travels in the United States. We have relied on Valérie Guillaume's chronology in *Jean Baudrillard et le Centre Pompidou: une biographie intellectuelle* (Lormont, 2013).

34 Lotringer, 'Untimely Meditations'.

35 Baudrillard, *Simulacra and Simulation*, p. 119.

36 Baudrillard, *The Mirror of Production*, p. 49.

37 Ibid., pp. 48–50.

38 Lotringer, 'Introduction: Domination and Servitude', p. 12.

39 Both of these were initially published as essays and later expanded into book form.

40 Jean Baudrillard, 'The Apathy of the Masses', interview with Pierre Boncenne and Alain Jaubert [1987], in *Jean Baudrillard: The Disappearance of Culture: Uncollected Interviews*, ed. Richard G. Smith and David B. Clarke (Edinburgh, 2017), pp. 66–79 (p. 70).

41 Didier Eribon, *Michel Foucault*, trans. Betsy Wing (Cambridge, MA, 1991), p. 275.

42 David Macey, *The Lives of Michel Foucault: A Biography* (Syracuse, NY, 1993), p. 360.

43 Lotringer, 'Untimely Meditations'.

44 Baudrillard, 'The Apathy of the Masses', pp. 69–70.

45 Eribon, *Michel Foucault*, p. 275.

46 Baudrillard, 'The Apathy of the Masses', p. 70.

47 Jean Baudrillard, 'Forget Artaud (Jean Baudrillard / Sylvère Lotringer)', in *The Conspiracy of Art*, trans. Ames Hodges (New York, 2005), pp. 217–36 (p. 223).

48 Baudrillard, 'The Apathy of the Masses', p. 70.

49 Baudrillard, 'Forget Artaud', p. 223.

50 Sylvère Lotringer, 'Introduction: Exterminating Angel', in Jean Baudrillard, *Forget Foucault*, trans. Nicole Dufresne (Los Angeles, CA, 1987), pp. 7–23 (p. 7).

51 Jean Baudrillard, *Passwords*, trans. Chris Turner (London, 2003), p. 21.

52 Jean Baudrillard, *Seduction*, trans. Brian Singer (Montréal, 1990), p. 57.

53 Baudrillard, 'The Apathy of the Masses', p. 67.

54 Baudrillard, 'Baudrillard's Seduction', p. 40.

55 Jean Baudrillard, *Fatal Strategies*, trans. Philip Beitchman and W.G.J. Niesluchowski (London, 1999), p. 100.

56 Ibid., p. 103.

57 Luce Irigaray, review of Baudrillard's *Seduction*, *Histoires d'elles* (21 March 1980).

58 Baudrillard, *Fatal Strategies*, p. 123.

59 Baudrillard, *America*, p. 70.

60 Jean Baudrillard, 'The Power of Reversibility that Exists in the Fatal', interview with D. Guillemot and D. Soutif [1983], in *Baudrillard Live*, ed. Gane, pp. 43–9 (p. 47).

61 Victoria Grace, *Baudrillard's Challenge: A Feminist Reading* (London, 2000).

4 Life on the Other Side: Art and America, 1980–86

1 Jean Baudrillard, *Simulacra and Simulation*, trans. Sheila Faria Glaser (Ann Arbor, MI, 1994), pp. 160–61.

2 Ibid., p. 1.

3 Ibid., p. 12.

4 Ibid., p. 79.

5 Ibid., p. 1.

6 Originally, 'Del rigor en la ciencia', and also translated as 'The Rigour of Science'.

7 Jorge Luis Borges, 'On Exactitude in Science', in *Collected Fictions*, trans. Andrew Hurley (New York, 1998), p. 325.

8 Jean Baudrillard, *Simulations*, trans. Paul Foss, Paul Patton and Philip Beitchman (New York, 1983), p. 2.

9 Ibid.

10 Ibid., p. 83.

11 Sylvère Lotringer, 'Introduction: Exterminating Angel', in Jean Baudrillard, *Forget Foucault*, trans. Nicole Dufresne (Los Angeles, CA, 1987), pp. 7–23 (p. 20).

12 Sylvère Lotringer, 'My '80s: Better than Life', *Artforum*, XLI/8 (April 2023), www.artforum.com.

13 Jean Baudrillard, *Fragments: Conversations with François L'Yvonnet*, trans. Chris Turner (London, 2004), p. 55.

14 Richard Hertz in Chris Kraus, 'This Is Chance', *Social Practices* (South Pasadena, CA, 2018), pp. 25–40 (p. 34).

15 Lotringer, 'My '80s: Better than Life'. Emphasis in original.

16 Sylvère Lotringer, 'La Théorie, mode d'emploi', *TLE*, 20 (Spring 2002), pp. 67–114 (p. 96).

17 Kraus, 'This Is Chance', p. 26.

18 Ibid.

19 François Cusset, *French Theory: How Foucault, Derrida, Deleuze, and Co. Transformed the Intellectual Life of the United States*, trans. Jeff Fort (Minneapolis, MN, 2008), p. 234.

20 Peter Halley, 'The Crisis in Geometry', *Arts Magazine*, LVIII/10 (June 1984), available at www.peterhalley.com/crisis-in-geometry.

21 Peter Schjeldahl quoted in Ben Davis, 'The New Gretchen Bender Survey Is a Triumph, Revealing a Visionary Artist – and a Tough Lesson about the Power of Media', *Artnet*, 26 April 2019, www.artnet.com.

22 Jean Baudrillard, 'Baudrillard's Seduction', interview with Patrice Bollon [1983], in *Baudrillard Live: Selected Interviews*, ed. Mike Gane (London, 1993), pp. 36–40 (p. 39).

23 Ibid.

24 Eva Wiseman, 'Sophie Calle: "What attracts me is absence, missing, death . . . "', *The Observer*, 2 July 2017, www.theguardian.com.

25 Sophie Calle, 'Sophie Calle in Conversation with Bice Curiger', in *Talking Art 1*, ed. Adrian Searle (London, 1993), pp. 29–42 (p. 30).

26 Jean Baudrillard, 'Please Follow Me', trans. Paul Foss, *Art and Text*, XXIII/4 (March–May 1987), pp. 103–14 (p. 105).

27 In his Introduction to Baudrillard's 1987 Semiotext(e) book *The Evil Demon of Images*, Alan Cholodenko cites the range of Australian art journals that were publishing essays by Baudrillard at the time as proof that 'his ideas have entered into common currency of cultural debate about the postmodern': Alan Cholodenko, Introduction to Jean Baudrillard, *The Evil Demon of Images*, trans. Paul Patton and Paul Foss (Los Angeles, CA, 1987), pp. 11–12 (p. 12).

28 Lotringer, 'My '80s: Better than Life'.

29 Jean Baudrillard, 'Untitled', in Barbara Kruger, *Barbara Kruger* (New York, 1987), n.p.

30 Cusset, *French Theory*, p. 238.

31 Lotringer, 'My '80s: Better than Life'.

32 Kraus, 'This Is Chance', p. 27.

33 Jean-Louis Violeau, 'Foreword: Baudrillard, the Ghost', in Jean Baudrillard, *The Ecstasy of Communication*, trans. Bernard Schütze and Caroline Schütze (South Pasadena, CA, 2012), pp. 9–16 (pp. 10–11).

34 Ibid., p. 12.

35 See the publisher's information for the new edition of The Ecstasy of Communication, translated by Bernard and Caroline Schütze, at https://mitpress.mit.edu, accessed 21 March 2025.

36 Peter Vorderer et al., *Permanently Online, Permanently Connected: Living and Communicating in a POPC World* (London, 2017).

37 Baudrillard, *The Ecstasy of Communication*, p. 20.

38 Ibid., p. 22.

5 'My own strange world': Baudrillard's Alternative 1980s

1 Jean Baudrillard, *Cool Memories II: 1987–1990*, trans. Chris Turner (Durham, NC, 1996), p. 7.

2 Jean Baudrillard, 'Strange World', interview with Nicholas Zurbrugg [1994], in *Jean Baudrillard: The Disappearance of Culture: Uncollected*

Interviews, ed. Richard G. Smith and David B. Clarke (Edinburgh, 2017), pp. 113–17 (p. 116).

3 Jean Baudrillard, 'The Apathy of the Masses', interview with Pierre Boncenne and Alain Jaubert [1987], in *The Disappearance of Culture*, ed. Smith and Clarke, pp. 66–79 (p. 68).

4 Jean Baudrillard, 'I Don't Belong to the Club, to the Seraglio', interview with Mike Gane and Monique Arnaud [1993], in *Baudrillard Live: Selected Interviews*, ed. Mike Gane (London, 1993), pp. 19–25 (p. 20).

5 Baudrillard, 'The Apathy of the Masses', p. 69.

6 Jean Baudrillard, 'Baudrillard's Seduction', interview with Patrice Bollon [1983], in *Baudrillard Live*, ed. Gane, pp. 36–40 (p. 39).

7 Baudrillard, 'I Don't Belong to the Club, to the Seraglio', p. 23.

8 Jean Baudrillard, 'Le Désert', radio interview on *France Culture* (6 March 1986), transcribed in *Jean Baudrillard et le Centre Pompidou: une biographie intellectuelle*, ed. Valérie Guillaume (Lormont, 2013), p. 110. Our translation.

9 Ibid., p. 111. Our translation.

10 Jean Baudrillard, 'L'Amérique comme fiction', interview with Jacques Henric and Guy Scarpetta [1986], in *Jean Baudrillard: entretiens 1968–2008*, ed. Laurent de Sutter (Paris, 2019), p. 181. Our translation. For 'pure travelling', see Jean Baudrillard, *America* [1986], trans. Chris Turner (London, 2010), p. 9.

11 Marine Baudrillard, communication to the authors.

12 Baudrillard, *America*, p. 66.

13 Baudrillard, 'L'Amérique comme fiction', p. 183. Our translation.

14 Baudrillard, 'Le Désert', p. 110. Our translation.

15 Ludovic Leonelli, *La Séduction Baudrillard* (Paris, 2007), pp. 13–14. Our translation.

16 Chris Kraus, 'This Is Chance', in *Social Practices* (South Pasadena, CA, 2018), pp. 25–40 (p. 29).

17 Baudrillard, *America*, p. 6.

18 Ibid., p. 5.

19 Ibid., p. 28.

20 Ibid., p. 32.

21 Baudrillard, 'Le Désert', p. 116. Our translation.

22 Baudrillard, *America*, p. 66.

23 Ibid., p. 29.

24 Ibid., p. 58.

25 Ibid.

26 Ibid., pp. 93, 7, 34.

27 Baudrillard, 'Le Désert', p. 116. Our translation.

28 Diane Rubenstein, 'America', in *The Baudrillard Dictionary*, ed. Richard G. Smith (Edinburgh, 2010), pp. 11–13 (p. 13).

29 Baudrillard, 'L'Amérique comme fiction', p. 178. Our translation.

30 Jean Baudrillard, *Fragments: Conversations with François L'Yvonnet*, trans. Chris Turner (London, 2004), p. 23.

31 Mike Gane, 'Fragments', in *The Baudrillard Dictionary*, ed. Smith, pp. 81–3 (p. 82).

32 Baudrillard, *Fragments*, p. 22.

33 Jean Baudrillard, *The Ecstasy of Communication*, trans. Bernard Schütze and Caroline Schütze (South Pasadena, CA, 2012), p. 28; Jean Baudrillard, *The Evil Demon of Images*, trans. Paul Patton and Paul Foss (Los Angeles, CA, 1987), pp. 18–19.

34 Jean Baudrillard, *Cool Memories IV: 1995–2000*, trans. Chris Turner (London, 2003), pp. 112–13.

35 Jean Baudrillard, *Cool Memories: 1980–1985*, trans. Chris Turner (London, 1990), p. 135.

36 Richard J. Lane, 'Cool Memories', in *The Baudrillard Dictionary*, ed. Smith, pp. 42–4 (p. 43). Lane is quoting from Baudrillard, *Cool Memories: 1980–1985*, p. 135.

37 Baudrillard, *Cool Memories*, p. 133.

38 Baudrillard, *Cool Memories II*, p. 13.

39 Jean Baudrillard, 'Too Bad about Patagonia', interview with Michel Jourde and Hadrien Laroche [1990], in *Jean Baudrillard: From Hyperreality to Disappearance: Uncollected Interviews*, ed. Richard G. Smith and David B. Clarke (Edinburgh, 2015), pp. 7–18 (p. 16).

40 Baudrillard, *Cool Memories II*, p. 26.

41 Leonelli, *La Séduction Baudrillard*, p. 123. Our translation.

42 Jean Baudrillard, *The Intelligence of Evil, or The Lucidity Pact*, trans. Chris Turner (London, 2013), p. 165.

43 Jean Baudrillard, 'For Illusion Isn't the Opposite of Reality . . . ', in *Photographies 1985–1998: Within the Horizon of the Object: Objects in This Mirror Are Closer than They Appear* (Ostfildern-Ruit, 1999), pp. 128–42 (p. 130).

44 Jean Baudrillard, 'Interview with Jean Baudrillard', in Paul Hegarty, *Jean Baudrillard: Live Theory* (London, 2004), pp. 134–49 (p. 142).

45 Jean Baudrillard, *Paroxysm: Interviews with Philippe Petit*, trans. Chris Turner (London and New York, 1998), pp. 99–100.

46 Jean Baudrillard, 'It is the Object Which Thinks Us', in *Photographies 1985–1998*, pp. 144–52.

47 Jean Baudrillard, *Fragments: Cool Memories III: 1991–1995* (Paris, 1995), p. 47. Our translation.

48 Baudrillard, *The Evil Demon of Images*, pp. 27–8. This book is the written version of the inaugural lecture for the Maria Kuttna Memorial Lecture on Film series Baudrillard was invited to give in Sydney, Australia, in 1984.

49 Ibid., p. 16.

50 Ibid., p. 18.

51 Baudrillard, 'For Illusion Isn't the Opposite of Reality . . . ', p. 140.

52 Ibid., p. 129.

53 Baudrillard, 'I Don't Belong to the Club, to the Seraglio', p. 23.

54 The exhibitions were at: the Neue Galerie, Graz, Austria, 1999; the Maison européenne de la photographie, Paris, 2001; the Biennale of Photography in Moscow, 2002; and the Kunsthalle Fridericianum in Kassel, Germany, in 2004. After Baudrillard died, exhibitions of his photography were staged at Vendôme, France (Promenades photographiques) in 2017; Dijon (Le Consortium museum) in 2018; Oxford Brookes University in 2018; Los Angeles (Château Shatto) in 2019; Shanghai (Power Station of Art) in 2019; and Montréal (Centre de design, Université du Québec à Montréal) in 2021.

55 Baudrillard, 'Strange World', p. 116.

6 Total Freedom, 1990–2004

1 Jean Baudrillard, 'This Beer Isn't a Beer', interview with Anne Laurent [1991], in *Baudrillard Live: Selected Interviews*, ed. Mike Gane (London, 1993), pp. 180–90 (p. 182).

2 Jean Baudrillard, 'The Apathy of the Masses', interview with Pierre Boncenne and Alain Jaubert [1987], in *Jean Baudrillard: The Disappearance of Culture: Uncollected Interviews*, ed. Richard G. Smith and David B. Clarke (Edinburgh, 2017), pp. 66–79 (p. 67).

3 Chris Turner, 'The Intelligence of Evil: An Introduction', in Jean Baudrillard, *The Intelligence of Evil, or The Lucidity Pact*, trans. Chris Turner (London, 2013), pp. 1–12 (p. 10).

4 Jean Baudrillard, *The Vital Illusion*, ed. Julia Witwer (New York, 2000), p. 57.

5 Jean Baudrillard, 'Baudrillard: The Interview', interview with Mike Gane and Monique Arnaud [1993], in *Baudrillard Live*, ed. Gane, pp. 199–207 (p. 203).

6   Tomasso Fagioli, Eleonora Conciliis and Nicholas Ruiz III, 'Reinventing the Real: A Conversation with Marine Dupuis Baudrillard', *Kritikos: An International and Interdisciplinary Journal of Postmodern Cultural Sound, Text and Image*, XV (Summer 2018), https://intertheory.org/marinebaudrillard.htm.

7   Ibid.

8   Baudrillard, *The Intelligence of Evil*, p. 13.

9   Jean Baudrillard, *Paroxysm: Interviews with Philippe Petit*, trans. Chris Turner (London and New York, 1998), p. 50.

10 Jean Baudrillard, *America*, trans. Chris Turner (London, 2010), p. 90.

11 Jean Baudrillard, 'Things Surpass Themselves', interview with Florian Rötzer [1995], in *Jean Baudrillard: From Hyperreality to Disappearance: Uncollected Interviews*, ed. Richard G. Smith and David B. Clarke (Edinburgh, 2015), pp. 95–108 (p. 106).

12 Jean Baudrillard, *The Transparency of Evil: Essays on Extreme Phenomena*, trans. James Benedict (London, 1993), pp. 7–8.

13 Jean Baudrillard, 'Anorexic Ruins', trans. David Antal, in *Looking Back on the End of the World*, ed. Dietmar Kamper and Christoph Wulf (Cambridge, MA, 1989), pp. 29–45.

14 Baudrillard, *Paroxysm*, pp. 9–10.

15 George Gerbner, 'Persian Gulf War: The Movie', in *Triumph of the Image: The Media's War in the Persian Gulf – A Global Perspective*, ed. Hamid Mowlana, George Gerbner and Herbert I. Schiller (Boulder, CO, 1992), pp. 243–65 (p. 252).

16 Jean Baudrillard, *Fragments: Cool Memories III: 1990–1995*, trans. Emily Agar (London, 1997), pp. 75–6.

17 The English translation appeared in 1995: Jean Baudrillard, *The Gulf War Did Not Take Place*, trans. Paul Patton (Sydney, 1995).

18 Brecht, as quoted by Baudrillard in *The Gulf War Did Not Take Place*, p. 81.

19 Baudrillard, 'This Beer Isn't a Beer', p. 180.

20 Christopher Norris, *Uncritical Theory: Postmodernism, Intellectuals and the Gulf War* (London, 1992).

21 Baudrillard, 'This Beer Isn't a Beer', p. 181.

22 Ibid.

23 Jean Baudrillard, 'The Roots of Evil', in *The Agony of Power*, trans. Ames Hodges (South Pasadena, CA, 2010), pp. 109–27 (p. 123).

24 Jean Baudrillard, in Caroline Bayard and Graham Knight, 'Vivisecting the 90s: An Interview with Jean Baudrillard' [1995], in *From Hyperreality to Disappearance*, ed. Smith and Clarke, pp. 76–94 (p. 79).

25 Baudrillard, 'The Apathy of the Masses', p. 70.

26 Fagioli, Conciliis and Ruiz, 'Reinventing the Real'.

27 Ibid.

28 Ibid.

29 Jean Baudrillard, *The Illusion of the End*, trans. Chris Turner (Cambridge, 1994), p. 43.

30 Jean Baudrillard, 'The End of the End', interview with John Johnston, in *Baudrillard Live*, ed. Gane, pp. 156–64 (p. 159).

31 Jean Baudrillard, 'I'm Not a Prophet', interview with Michael Fordham [1997], in *From Hyperreality to Disappearance*, ed. Smith and Clarke, pp. 113–21 (p. 117). Emphasis in original.

32 Baudrillard, 'The Apathy of the Masses', p. 78.

33 Jean Baudrillard, 'Intellectuals, Commitment and Political Power', interview with Maria Shevtsova (1985), in *Baudrillard Live*, ed. Gane, pp. 72–80 (p. 79).

34 Jean Baudrillard, 'Pas de pitié pour Sarajevo', *Libération*, 6 January 1994, pp. 13–16.

35 Evans Chan, 'Against Postmodernism, etcetera – A Conversation with Susan Sontag', *Postmodern Culture*, 901 (2001), https://pmc.iath. virginia.edu, accessed 10 January 2025.

36 Jean Baudrillard, 'La Commedia dell'Arte', interview with Catherine Francblin [1996], in *The Disappearance of Culture*, ed. Smith and Clarke, pp. 129–36 (p. 130).

37 Ibid., p. 136.

38 Jean Baudrillard. 'Hate: A Last Sign of Life', interview with François Ewald [1999], in *The Disappearance of Culture*, ed. Smith and Clarke, pp. 132–42 (p. 137).

39 Baudrillard, *Paroxysm*, p. 11.

40 Jean Baudrillard, 'Aesthetic Illusion and Virtual Reality', in *Jean Baudrillard: Art and Artefact*, ed. Nicholas Zurbrugg (London, 1997), pp. 19–27 (p. 24).

41 Chris Kraus, 'This Is Chance', in *Social Practices* (South Pasadena, CA, 2018), pp. 25–40 (p. 27).

42 Ludovic Leonelli, *La Séduction Baudrillard* (Paris, 2007), p. 51. Our translation.

43 Fagioli, Conciliis and Ruiz, 'Reinventing the Real'.

44 Kraus, 'This Is Chance', p. 30.

45 Ibid., p. 35.

46 In her essay about the event, 'This Is Chance', published in 2018 – to which much of this account is indebted – Kraus lists some of these:

'Self-Hatred and the Resentment of Freedom, or, Individuality as a Betrayal of Space'; 'Fatal Experimentation on Oneself in Place of Extinct Destiny'; 'The Fractal Subject, or, Self-Empowerment to the Point of Self-Destruction'; 'The Continental Divide, or The Division of Our Mental Divide, or The Sharing of Our Destinies'; 'Plural and Parallel Worlds and the Difficulty of Dying Everywhere at the Same Time'; 'Devolution of Transference of the Will, and The All-Powerful Game of Nostalgia for the World We Think'. Ibid., pp. 25–6.

47 François Cusset, *French Theory: How Foucault, Derrida, Deleuze, and Co. Transformed the Intellectual Life of the United States*, trans. Jeff Fort (Minneapolis, MN, 2008), p. 73.

48 Kraus, 'This Is Chance', p. 33.

49 Jean Baudrillard, 'The Conspiracy of Art' [1996], in *The Conspiracy of Art*, trans. Ames Hodges (New York, 2005), pp. 25–9.

50 Andrew Hultkrans, 'Three Days in the Desert', *Artforum* (January 1997), www.artforum.com.

51 William Merrin, '"Did You Ever Eat Tasty Wheat?": Baudrillard and *The Matrix*', *Scope: An Online Journal of Film and Television Studies* (May 2003), available at www.nottingham.ac.uk.

52 Cusset, *French Theory*, p. 259.

53 Jean Baudrillard, in '*The Matrix* Decoded: *Le Nouvel Observateur* Interview with Jean Baudrillard', *International Journal of Baudrillard Studies*, 1/2 (July 2004), available at https://baudrillardstudies.ubishops.ca.

54 Jean Baudrillard, 'Impossible and Unexchangeable', interview with Paul Hegarty [2004], in *The Disappearance of Culture*, ed. Smith and Clarke, pp. 194–209 (p. 201).

55 Baudrillard, in Bayard and Knight, 'Vivisecting the 90s', p. 88.

56 Baudrillard, *The Vital Illusion*, p. 52.

57 Baudrillard, 'Impossible and Unexchangeable', p. 200.

58 Kraus, 'This Is Chance', p. 26.

59 Baudrillard, *Paroxysm*, p. 35.

60 A different version of the book, including essays in the English and French editions of *The Spirit of Terrorism*, was also published by Éditions Galilée in 2002 as *Power Inferno* (title originally in English).

61 Jean Baudrillard, *The Spirit of Terrorism and Other Essays*, trans. Chris Turner (London, 2002), p. 17.

62 Jean Baudrillard, *Simulacra and Simulation*, trans. Sheila Faria Glaser (Ann Arbor, MI, 1994), p. 163.

63 Jean Baudrillard, 'This Is the Fourth World War', interview with Romain Leick [2002], in *From Hyperreality to Disappearance*, ed. Smith and Clarke (Edinburgh, 2015), pp. 171–8 (p. 173).

64 Ibid., pp. 171–2.

65 From the radio programme *Tout arrive* on the public radio channel *France Culture* in May 2004: Turner, 'The Intelligence of Evil: An Introduction', p. 10.

66 Baudrillard, *The Intelligence of Evil*, p. 168.

Conclusion: Beyond

1 Jean Baudrillard, *Cool Memories: 1980–1985*, trans. Chris Turner (London, 1990), p. 24.

 2 Marine Baudrillard, in Tomasso Fagioli, Eleonora Conciliis and Nicholas Ruiz III, 'Reinventing the Real: A Conversation with Marine Dupuis Baudrillard', *Kritikos: An International and Interdisciplinary Journal of Postmodern Cultural Sound, Text and Image*, XV (Summer 2018), https://intertheory.org/marinebaudrillard.htm.

 3 Jean Baudrillard, *Cool Memories II: 1987–1990*, trans. Chris Turner (Durham, NC, 1996), p. 83.

 4 Steven Poole, 'Obituary: Jean Baudrillard', *The Guardian*, 7 March 2007, www.theguardian.com.

 5 Jean Baudrillard, *Paroxysm: Interviews with Philippe Petit*, trans. Chris Turner (London and New York, 1998), p. 61.

 6 Peter Gente, 'Jean Baudrillard and the Arts: A Tribute to His 75th Birthday', https://zkm.de, accessed 20 March 2025.

 7 Chris Kraus, 'This Is Chance', in *Social Practices* (South Pasadena, CA, 2018), pp. 25–40 (p. 29).

 8 Fagioli, Conciliis and Ruiz, 'Reinventing the Real'.

 9 Joseph Nechvatal, 'Fine Absurdist Ubu Art: Review of Jean Baudrillard, "Pataphysics"', *International Journal of Baudrillard Studies*, IV/1 (January 2007), available at https://post.thing.net.

10 Jean Baudrillard, 'Forget Artaud (Jean Baudrillard / Sylvère Lotringer)', in *The Conspiracy of Art*, trans. Ames Hodges (New York, 2005), pp. 217–36 (p. 217).

11 Subsequent references to obituaries of Baudrillard included in Robert J. Antonio, 'The Passing of Jean Baudrillard', *Fast Capitalism*, IV/1 (2007), pp. 161–71.

12 Fagioli, Conciliis and Ruiz, 'Reinventing the Real'.

13 Sylvère Lotringer, 'Untimely Meditations: On Jean Baudrillard', *Artforum* (2007), https://baudrillardstudies.ubishops.ca.

14 Ibid.

15 Jean Baudrillard and Truls Lie, 'The Art of Disappearing', 7 April 2007, *Eurozine*, www.eurozine.com.

16 Jean-Michel Rabaté, *The Future of Theory* (Oxford, 2002), p. 9.

17 Jacques Donzelot, 'Patasociology at the University of Nanterre', *Cultural Politics*, VII/3 (2011), pp. 359–70.

18 Jean Baudrillard, *Impossible Exchange*, trans. Chris Turner (London, 2001), p. 151.

19 Lunenfeld quoted in Kraus, 'This Is Chance', p. 33.

20 Jean Baudrillard, 'Too Bad about Patagonia', interview with Michel Jourde and Hadrien Laroche [1990], in *Jean Baudrillard: From Hyperreality to Disappearance: Uncollected Interviews*, ed. Richard G. Smith and David B. Clarke (Edinburgh, 2015), pp. 7–18 (p. 16).

21 Jean Baudrillard, *Why Hasn't Everything Already Disappeared?*, trans. Chris Turner (Brighton, 2016), p. 9.

22 Ibid., p. 20.

23 Ibid., p. 21.

24 Ibid., p. 25.

25 Marina Benjamin, 'The Philosopher Clown', *Prospect*, 19 July 1997, www.prospectmagazine.co.uk.

26 Jean Baudrillard, *Cool Memories IV: 1995–2000*, trans. Chris Turner (London, 2003), p. 98.

27 Baudrillard, *Why Hasn't Everything Already Disappeared?*, pp. 25–6.

28 Jean-Louis Violeau, 'Foreword: Baudrillard, the Ghost', in Jean Baudrillard, *The Ecstasy of Communication*, trans. Bernard Schütze and Caroline Schütze (South Pasadena, CA, 2012), pp. 9–16 (p. 15).

29 Jean Baudrillard, *Fragments: Conversations with François L'Yvonnet*, trans. Chris Turner (London, 2004), p. 73.

30 Jean Baudrillard, *Screened Out*, trans. Chris Turner (London, 2014), p. 193.

31 Baudrillard, *Paroxysm*, p. 50.

32 Jean Baudrillard, *The Transparency of Evil: Essays on Extreme Phenomena*, trans. James Benedict (London, 1993), p. 23.

33 Baudrillard, *Why Hasn't Everything Already Disappeared?*, p. 33.

34 Ibid., p. 34.

35 Baudrillard, *Cool Memories IV*, p. 7.

36 Baudrillard, *Why Hasn't Everything Already Disappeared?*, pp. 63–4.

37 Ibid., p. 64.

38 Baudrillard, *Fragments*, p. 71.

Select Bibliography

By Baudrillard: Books in English
Baudrillard's books are listed in order of original publication. The translated editions referred to are those we have used in this volume and, where they differ, the original French publication dates are in square brackets.

The System of Objects [1968], trans. James Benedict (London, 2005)
The Consumer Society: Myths and Structures [1970], trans. Chris Turner (London, 1998)
For a Critique of the Political Economy of the Sign [1972], trans. Charles Levin (London, 2019)
The Mirror of Production [1973], trans. Mark Poster (St Louis, MO, 1975)
Symbolic Exchange and Death [1976], trans. Iain Hamilton Grant (London, 1993)
Forget Foucault [1977], trans. Nicole Dufresne (Los Angeles, CA, 1987)
In the Shadow of the Silent Majorities [1978], trans. Paul Foss, Paul Patton and John Johnston (New York, 1983)
Seduction [1979], trans. Brian Singer (Montréal, 1990)
Simulacra and Simulation [1981], trans. Sheila Faria Glaser (Ann Arbor, MI, 1994)
Sophie Calle and Jean Baudrillard, *Suite vénetienne / Please Follow Me* [1983], trans. Dany Barash and Danny Hatfield (Seattle, WA, 1988)
Simulations, trans. Paul Foss, Paul Patton and Philip Beitchman (New York, 1983)
Fatal Strategies [1983], trans. Philip Beitchman and W.G.J. Niesluchowski (London, 1990)
The Divine Left: A Chronicle of the Years, 1977–1984 [1985], trans. David L. Sweet (Los Angeles, CA, 2014)
America [1986], trans. Chris Turner (London, 2010)
The Evil Demon of Images, trans. Paul Patton and Paul Foss (Los Angeles, CA, 1987)

The Ecstasy of Communication [1987], trans. Bernard Schütze and Caroline
  Schütze (South Pasadena, CA, 2012)
Cool Memories: 1980–1985 [1987], trans. Chris Turner (London, 1990)
Selected Writings [1988], edited and introduced by Mark Poster, 2nd edn
  (Cambridge, 2001)
*Revenge of the Crystal: Selected Writings on the Modern Object and Its Destiny,
  1968–1983*, trans. Paul Foss and Julian Pefanis (London, 1990)
The Transparency of Evil: Essays on Extreme Phenomena [1990], trans. James
  Benedict (London, 1993)
Cool Memories II: 1987–1990 [1990], trans. Chris Turner (Durham, NC, 1996)
The Gulf War Did Not Take Place [1991], trans. Paul Patton (Sydney, 1995)
The Illusion of the End [1992], trans. Chris Turner (Cambridge, 1994)
Jean Baudrillard and Marc Guillame [1994/8], *Radical Alterity*, trans. Ames
  Hodges (New York, 2008)
The Perfect Crime [1995], trans. Chris Turner (London, 1996)
Fragments: Cool Memories III: 1990–1995 [1995], trans. Emily Agar (London, 1997)
*Photographies 1985–1998: Within the Horizon of the Object: Objects in This
  Mirror Are Closer than They Appear* (Ostfildern-Ruit, 1999)
Impossible Exchange [1999], trans. Chris Turner (London, 2001)
The Vital Illusion, ed. Julia Witwer (New York, 2000)
Screened Out [2000], trans. Chris Turner (London, 2002)
Jean Baudrillard and Jean Nouvel, *The Singular Objects of Architecture*
  [2000], trans. Robert Bononno (Minneapolis, MN, 2002)
Cool Memories IV: 1995–2000 [2000], trans. Chris Turner (New York, 2003)
Passwords [2000], trans. Chris Turner (London, 2003)
The Uncollected Baudrillard, ed. Gary Genosko (London, 2001)
Telemorphosis [2001], trans. Drew S. Burk (Minneapolis, MN, 2012)
The Spirit of Terrorism and Other Essays, trans. Chris Turner (London, 2002)
The Intelligence of Evil, or The Lucidity Pact [2004], trans. Chris Turner
  (London, 2013)
The Conspiracy of Art, trans. Ames Hodges (New York, 2005)
Cool Memories V: 2000–2004 [2005], trans. Chris Turner (Oxford, 2006)
Jean Baudrillard and Enrique Valiente Noailles, *Exiles from Dialogue* [2005],
  trans. Chris Turner (Cambridge, 2007)
Utopia Deferred: Writings from 'Utopie' (1967–1978), trans. Stuart Kendall
  (New York, 2006)
Why Hasn't Everything Already Disappeared? [2007], trans. Chris Turner
  (Brighton, 2016)
The Agony of Power, trans. Ames Hodges (South Pasadena, CA, 2010)
Carnival and Cannibal: Ventriloquous Evil (London, 2010)

With Baudrillard: Interviews

Mike Gane, ed., *Baudrillard Live: Selected Interviews* (London, 1993)

Jean Baudrillard, *Paroxysm: Interviews with Philippe Petit*, trans. Chris Turner (London, 1998)

Jean Baudrillard, 'The Transparency of Kitsch: A Conversation with Enrico Baj', in *The Uncollected Baudrillard*, ed. Gary Genosko (London, 2001), pp. 143–54

Jean Baudrillard, *Fragments: Conversations with François L'Yvonnet*, trans. Chris Turner (London, 2004)

Jean Baudrillard, 'Forget Artaud (Jean Baudrillard / Sylvère Lotringer)', in *The Conspiracy of Art*, trans. Ames Hodges (New York, 2005), pp. 217–36

Jean Baudrillard, 'The Roots of Evil', in *The Agony of Power*, trans. Ames Hodges (South Pasadena, CA, 2010), pp. 109–27

Richard G. Smith and David B. Clarke, ed., *Jean Baudrillard: From Hyperreality to Disappearance: Uncollected Interviews* (Edinburgh, 2015)

Richard G. Smith and David B. Clarke, ed., *Jean Baudrillard: The Disappearance of Culture: Uncollected Interviews* (Edinburgh, 2017)

About Baudrillard: Selected Books, Essays and Interviews

Bishop, Ryan, ed., *Baudrillard Now: Current Perspectives in Baudrillard Studies* (Cambridge, 2009)

Butler, Rex, *Jean Baudrillard: The Defence of the Real* (London, 1999)

Butterfield, Bradley, 'The Baudrillardian Symbolic, 9/11, and the War of Good and Evil', *Postmodern Culture*, XIII/1 (2002), www.pomoculture.org

—, 'Ethical Value and Negative Aesthetics: Reconsidering the Baudrillard– Ballard Connection', *PMLA*, CXIV/1 (1999), pp. 64–77

Cholodenko, Alan, 'Introduction', in Jean Baudrillard, *The Evil Demon of Images*, trans. Paul Patton and Paul Foss (Los Angeles, CA, 1987)

Clarke, David B., et al., *Jean Baudrillard: Fatal Theories* (London, 2009)

Constable, Catherine, *Adapting Philosophy: Jean Baudrillard and 'The Matrix'* (Manchester, 2009)

Coulter, Gerry, *Jean Baudrillard: From the Ocean to the Desert, or the Poetics of Radicality* (Skyland, NC, 2014)

Donzelot, Jacques, 'Patasociology at the University of Nanterre', *Cultural Politics*, VII/3 (2011), pp. 359–70

Evans, Mihail, *The Singular Politics of Derrida and Baudrillard* (London, 2014)

Fagioli, Tomasso, Eleonora Conciliis and Nicholas Ruiz III, 'Reinventing the Real: A Conversation with Marine Dupuis Baudrillard', *Kritikos*, XV (Summer 2018), https://intertheory.org/marinebaudrillard.htm

Gane, Mike, *Baudrillard: Critical and Fatal Theory* (New York, 1991)
—, *Baudrillard's Bestiary: Baudrillard and Culture* (London, 1991)
—, *Jean Baudrillard: In Radical Uncertainty* (London, 2000)
Genosko, Gary, *Baudrillard and Signs: Signification Ablaze* (London, 1994)
—, *McLuhan and Baudrillard: Masters of Implosion* (London, 1999)
—, 'No More Models: Baudrillard's Critique of Communication', *Cultural Politics*, VII/3 (2011), pp. 409–30
Grace, Victoria, *Baudrillard's Challenge: A Feminist Reading* (London, 2000)
Guillaume, Valérie, ed., *Jean Baudrillard et le Centre Pompidou: une biographie intellectuelle* (Lormont, 2013)
Gunderson, Ryan, and Stephen Dobson, *Baudrillard's Journey to America* (London, 1996)
Hegarty, Paul, *Jean Baudrillard: Live Theory* (London, 2004)
Horrocks, Chris, *Baudrillard and the Millennium* (Cambridge, 1999)
Kellner, Douglas, *Jean Baudrillard: From Marxism to Postmodernism and Beyond* (Cambridge, 1989)
Khandizaji, Amirhosein, *Baudrillard and the Culture Industry: Returning to the First Generation of the Frankfurt School* (London, 2018)
Kline, Kip, *Baudrillard, Youth, and American Film: Fatal Theory and Education* (Edinburgh, 2016)
Kraus, Chris, 'This Is Chance', in *Social Practices* (South Pasadena, CA, 2018), pp. 25–40
Lane, Richard J., *Jean Baudrillard* (London, 2000)
—, 'Obituary: Jean Baudrillard', *Radical Philosophy*, 144 (July/August 2007), www.radicalphilosophy.com
Leonelli, Ludovic, *La Séduction Baudrillard* (Paris, 2007)
Levin, Charles, *Jean Baudrillard: A Study in Cultural Metaphysics* (London, 1996)
Lotringer, Sylvère, 'Introduction: Exterminating Angel', in Jean Baudrillard, *Forget Foucault*, trans. Nicole Dufresne (Los Angeles, CA, 1987), pp. 7–23
—, 'Untimely Meditations: On Jean Baudrillard', *Artforum* (2007), https://baudrillardstudies.ubishops.ca
Macey, David, 'Obituary: Jean Baudrillard', *Radical Philosophy*, 144 (July/August 2007), pp. 61–6
McQueen, Sean, *Deleuze and Baudrillard: From Cyberpunk to Biopunk* (Edinburgh, 2016)
Merrin, William, *Baudrillard and the Media* (Cambridge, 2005)
—, '"Did You Ever Eat Tasty Wheat?": Baudrillard and *The Matrix*', *Scope* (2003), www.nottingham.ac.uk/scope/documents/2003/may-2003/merrin.pdf

Nicol, Bran, 'Detective Fiction and "The Original Crime": Baudrillard, Calle, Poe', *Cultural Politics*, VII/3 (2011), pp. 445–64

Pawlett, William, *Jean Baudrillard: Against Banality* (London, 2007)

—, *Violence, Society and Radical Theory: Bataille, Baudrillard and Contemporary Society* (Farnham, 2013)

Pefanis, Julian, *Heterology and the Postmodern: Bataille, Baudrillard, and Lyotard* (Durham, NC, 1991)

Proto, Francesco, *Baudrillard for Architects* (London, 2019)

Rajan, Tilottama, *Deconstruction and the Remainders of Phenomenology: Sartre, Derrida, Foucault, Baudrillard* (Stanford, CA, 2002)

Rizza, Michael James, *The Topographical Imagination of Jameson, Baudrillard, and Foucault* (Aurora, CO, 2015)

Rojek, Chris, and Bryan Turner, eds, *Forget Baudrillard* (London, 1993)

Rubenstein, Diane, '"The Conspiracy of Imbeciles", Reloaded: Baudrillard and the DSK Affair', *Cultural Politics*, X/1 (2014), pp. 40–61

—, 'This Is Not a President: Baudrillard, Bush, and Enchanted Simulation', in *The Hysterical Male: New Feminist Theories*, ed. Arthur Kroker and Marilouise Kroker (New York, 1991), pp. 253–65

Schuster, Marc, *Don DeLillo, Jean Baudrillard, and the Consumer Conundrum* (Amherst, NY, 2008)

Scott, David H. T., *Semiologies of Travel: From Gautier to Baudrillard* (Cambridge, 2004)

Smith, Richard G., ed., *The Baudrillard Dictionary* (Edinburgh, 2010)

Stearns, William, and William Chaloupka, eds, *Jean Baudrillard: The Disappearance of Art and Politics* (Basingstoke, 1992)

Toffoletti, Kim, *Baudrillard Reframed: Interpreting Key Thinkers for the Arts* (London, 2011)

Violeau, Jean-Louis, 'Foreword: Baudrillard, the Ghost', in Jean Baudrillard, *The Ecstasy of Communication*, trans. Bernard Schütze and Caroline Schütze (South Pasadena, CA, 2012), pp. 9–16

Walters, James, *Baudrillard and Theology* (London, 2012)

Wilcox, Leonard, 'Baudrillard, September 11, and the Haunting Abyss of Reversal', *Postmodern Culture*, XIV/1 (2003), https://dx.doi.org/10.1353/pmc.2003.0042

Zurbrugg, Nicholas, ed., *Jean Baudrillard: Art and Artefact* (London, 1997)

The *International Journal of Baudrillard Studies* is a valuable online resource containing many essays and articles on Baudrillard: https://baudrillardstudies.ubishops.ca.

Acknowledgements

The authors would like to thank: Marine Baudrillard, Camille Zéhenne, Katharina Niemeyer, Antoine Lannegrand, Sophie Corbillé, Marie Gryczynski, Sylvia Almeida, Lionel Fantin, Agnès Le Baube, Charlotte Devai, Patricia Pulham, Jo Plaistowe and all of our colleagues and friends who helped with discussions, support and encouragement.

Photo Acknowledgements

The authors and publishers wish to express their thanks to the sources listed below for illustrative material and/or permission to reproduce it. Some locations of artworks are also given below, in the interest of brevity.

Alamy: pp. 37 (BNA Photographic), 45 (Associated Press), 49 (Photo 12), 68 (booksR), 88 (Sueddeutsche Zeitung Photo); authors' collection: p. 12; with the kind authorization of Marine Baudrillard (all images © Marine Baudrillard): pp. 51, 71, 81, 100, 104, 112, 113, 114, 133, 145, 147; Bibliothèque Municipale de la ville de Reims: p. 30; Bridgeman Images: pp. 8 (© Louis Monier. All rights reserved 2024), 15 (IMAGO/Detlev Konnerth), 43 (Photo © AGIP), 61 (© Louis Monier. All rights reserved 2024), 84 (© Sophie Bassouls. All rights reserved 2024), 118 (© Marion Kalter. All rights reserved 2024); Creative Commons: pp. 23 (Public Domain), 26 (CC BY-SA 4.0), 131 (Evil Vegeta/CC BY 2.0); Gallimard via Opale Photo: pp. 40, 64; thanks to Alex Van Gelder for allowing reproduction: p. 142; © Jo Plaistowe: p. 89.